WHO DOES WHAT BY HOW MUCH?

A PRACTICAL GUIDE TO CUSTOMER-CENTRIC OKRs

JEFF GOTHELF & JOSH SEIDEN

Authors of **Sense & Respond**

Publisher: Sense & Respond Press.
Copyright © 2024, Jeff Gothelf & Josh Seiden
ISBN 978-1-7328184-4-6 (paper)
ISBN 978-1-7328184-5-3 (ebook)

Contents

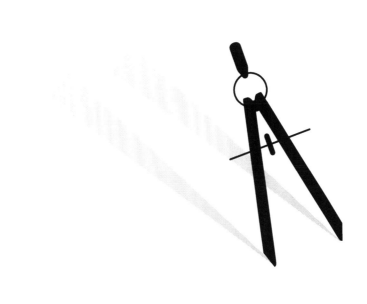

Introduction

Every organization wants to get better.

At least, every organization that we've ever worked with, and we've worked with many of them. We—Jeff and Josh—have worked with hundreds of organizations as individual contributors, leaders, founders, and consultants. We've seen firsthand how organizations of all kinds—good ones, bad ones, profitable ones, not-so-profitable ones—share an earnest desire to improve their work, improve *how* they work, and improve *the results* they get from their hard work.

And to be clear, pretty much everyone we've worked with works hard. So, the organizations we work with aren't worried about people working hard enough. They're worried that **people are working hard but working on the wrong stuff**. And this problem—people working on the wrong stuff—cuts across every organization: big, small, public, private, for-profit, not-for-profit, government, and private sector. People waste an enormous amount of time, money, and energy working on the wrong things.

We've spent most of our careers helping organizations solve this problem and discovered some powerful ways to do so. OKRs are one of the best ways we've found to get people working together on **the right stuff**. That's what this book is all about.

What's the Problem?

Before we get to the solution, let's look at the problem: **Why *do* people work on the wrong stuff?** Are they stupid? Lazy? Are their bosses idiots? In most cases, no—despite what you might read on LinkedIn or what you might think sometimes—that's not it.

The most common reason people work on the wrong stuff is that **they lose track of what their customers want**.

Organizations exist to provide some kind of value to people. In this book, we call these people "customers." In your organization, you might call them something else: constituents, students, patients, citizens, or even coworkers. Whatever term you use, the point is that we're all generally in the business of serving other people's needs. Too often, though, organizations don't have a clear understanding of *who* these people are or *what* they need.

There are other big problems, of course: alignment, collaboration, strategy, focus. These things are hard to create, hard to agree on, and hard to execute. Usually, teams face challenges that are some combination of *all of the above.*

In the early days of our careers as software designers, we worked on that first problem—how to help organizations be more customer-centric. In fact, that's how we met, in the design community in New York City. But as much as we loved design, we both came to understand that design is a means to an end. Our real passion was helping people—at first small teams, then larger organizations—collaborate effectively to get better results. We love to see teams doing great work. We love to see organizations thriving. Eventually, our journeys, both together and individually, led us to Objectives and Key Results, or OKRs.

In OKRs, we found a tool that has the ability to align teams around customer needs and focus them on company strategy. OKRs create clarity, help with prioritization, and, most of all, help teams deliver results. OKRs also work as a management tool uniquely suited to this moment in time—a time of great change and disruption, a time that requires continuous learning and agility.

Why This Book?

The book that you're reading now almost didn't exist. After all, there are many other books on OKRs, and we debated whether the world needed another one. But the more we looked at those books, the more we realized that we had to write our own. Because as good as some of those books are, they are missing something that we think is important: the idea that **everyone—yes, *everyone*—has a customer.**

Now look, you might disagree with that statement, but stick with us for a minute because we think we can convince you it's true. And once we do, we think you'll stick with us for the rest of this book.

Everyone Has a Customer

For the purposes of this book, when we refer to "customers," we mean the people who consume the things that you make at work. These people might be end customers in the classic sense of the word, but they might be people closer to you: They might be your colleagues in another part of the office.

When we talk about "customer behavior," we mean the actions that these people take. We're particularly interested in the actions that they take in response to the work that you're doing.

Customer Behavior = Results

Speaking of the actions they take...**your success depends on how these people—your customers—respond to your work**. Do end customers buy more of your products? Do they subscribe to your newsletter? Do they refer your services to their friends and colleagues?

If you're thinking about internal customers, we can ask the same kind of questions: Do your coworkers use the presentation you create? Do they adopt the plans you propose?

Those are indications of whether or not your work is valuable. If it works for your customers, it means better business results for you.

Who Does What by How Much?

"Who does what by how much?" is, in a nutshell, your value equation. It has three parts.

- "Who?" is your customer.
- "Does what?" is their behavior.
- "By how much?" is the measure of change in their behavior.

Focus your work on identifying and tracking all three, and you've won half the battle.

OKRs and the Value Equation

OKRs, if you use them correctly, are built around this value equation. Objectives are your high-level goal statement. Key results are your measures of success, which we write using our simple value equation: *who does what by how much?*

In other words, OKRs are built around a set of questions: If we're going to achieve our goal, who are the people we serve, what do they want to do, how can we help them, and how can we quantify this?

These questions give you customer-centricity. They provide focus and clarity. And they are deeply practical.

Older management systems made the assumption that organizational leaders knew the answers to these questions at the start of every project. But as we said above, people are complex and unpredictable (and, OK, wonderful). That means that we usually *don't* know these answers. To deal with this, we need a way forward that helps us figure out these answers and that unlocks the smarts of *everyone* in the organization. Objectives and key results are that way forward.

Making Things Simple and Clear

We've seen many explanations of OKRs and worked with many people to teach and coach the method. We've experimented with multiple ways to communicate our ideas. When we started talking about *Who Does What by How Much*, we were delighted to get this feedback from a commenter on LinkedIn: "This was the clearest explanation of OKRs I've ever heard."

Ultimately, that's our goal with this book: to share this method with you in the clearest way possible, so you can put these ideas to work immediately and start improving your organization.

About Us

We're Jeff Gothelf and Josh Seiden, two software designers turned coaches, consultants, and speakers who help organizations fuse strategy, customer-centricity, and evidence-based decision-making to become more agile (with a lowercase "a"), make better products, and achieve greater success.

We have worked as a team for years and have co-written two books before this one: the award-winning *Lean UX* (now in its third edition) and *Sense & Respond*, published by Harvard Business Review Press and nominated for a Thinkers50 distinction in Innovation. Josh is also the author of *Outcomes vs. Output*, and Jeff is the author of *Lean vs. Agile vs. Design Thinking* and *Forever Employable*.

What This Book Is

Who Does What by How Much? is a how-to guide for using OKRs and how they change the way you work, regardless of your role, team, or organization.

It's a manual for understanding who your customers are, how your work affects what your customers do, and how all of that will create results that matter—to you, your team, and your organization.

This book is a practical handbook for you, no matter where you sit in your organization.

OKRs Aren't Just for Tech Teams

OKRs grew up in the tech world, beginning at Intel and gaining notice at Google, and much of what you'll find about OKRs has a strong tech bias. **But this book is not only for tech teams.** We've used OKRs well beyond tech. OKRs work anywhere that teams face challenging questions and uncertainty—which we think is pretty much everywhere.

Let's say this clearly: OKRs are valuable in any industry. This book assumes that you, our reader, could be working in any kind of organization, in any sector, and on any kind of problem.

How to Use This Book

We've broken the book down into four parts:

1. What Are OKRs?
2. How to Create OKRs
3. How to Use OKRs
4. How to Make OKRs Successful in Your Organization

In Part 1, we'll introduce the idea of OKRs and share their key concepts. If you're new to OKRs, you definitely want to start here. If you already have experience with OKRs, this first part of the book will help you understand how our approach differs from other approaches to OKRs.

Part 2 is an instruction manual for creating OKRs. There, you'll find detailed processes that you can use to work through the OKR-creation process with your team.

Part 3 is the instruction manual for *using* OKRs. Once you've written OKRs, you'll want to put them in motion. You do that with something called the OKR Cycle. Part 3 is all about the OKRs and how to use them to improve your work. There, we talk about planning work, doing work, and coordinating work, all through the lens of OKRs.

In Part 4, we describe the key success factors for ensuring OKRs work well in your organization, including the implications for leadership, management, and culture.

Feel free to skip around. If you already have some level of comfort and experience with OKRs, you may want to dive right into some of the later chapters. If you're a total OKR newcomer, we encourage you to start at the very beginning.

The most important things to remember as you read and use this book are: **Your work creates value. It creates value for other people. Those people are your customers. Your customers' behaviors are what drive results for your organization. OKRs help you target those behaviors.**

Got it? Don't worry, we'll repeat the idea many times. Now, let's get started.

Part 1

What Are OKRs?

This first part of the book is about the fundamentals of OKRs.

We'll define OKRs and show you some examples. We'll share our unique point of view on what makes OKRs powerful and customer-centric. Then, we'll focus on the benefits you can expect to see if you implement OKRs correctly.

We'll share some key principles that can guide your implementation of OKRs. You can use these principles to reflect on *why* you want to use OKRs and how you can use them to improve how you work.

Finally, we'll talk about one of the most important ideas at the center of OKRs: outcomes. Understanding this idea is critical for using OKRs effectively.

Let's dive in.

Chapter 1

What Are OKRs?

Last year, we received an email from Monica, who works in the human resources department of a major U.S.-based shoe company. "Our team here wants to do OKRs," she wrote, "but our company makes shoes. What does that mean for us?"

You may be asking yourself the same question. Objectives and Key Results (OKRs) are a popular goal-setting framework that many people associate with the tech world. They were born at Intel, made famous by Google, and are widely used by tech companies. But OKRs are a powerful set of tools that can be (and are being) used by organizations of all shapes and sizes—certainly by tech startups and giants, but also by nonprofits, hospital systems, and even, as you'll see, shoe companies.

The shoe company where Monica works has created iconic and innovative shoe brands—brands that are household names around the world. Despite their innovative products, the company's leaders wanted to improve the way the company worked. They had heard about OKRs and wondered if they could use them successfully.

They could. And so can you.

No matter your industry or the size of your organization, OKRs can help you become more successful. OKRs have the ability to focus your work on delivering value to customers. They also create the agility to adjust course quickly when customer needs change. Finally, they create the alignment and transparency people in modern organizations require to do great work. These things are crucial to the success of *all* organizations.

What Are OKRs?

In some ways, OKRs are simple. We can teach the OKR framework itself in just a few minutes—and that simplicity is one of the things that makes OKRs so compelling. The framework isn't the only piece of the OKR puzzle, though; there are three pieces to implementing OKRs:

1. a simple but powerful goal-setting framework
2. a set of processes for using OKRs
   and getting work done
3. a culture that OKRs have the potential to
   create and that they require in order for
   organizations using them to thrive.

Let's start with the core of OKRs: the goal-setting framework.

OKRs Are a Goal-Setting Framework

Objectives and Key Results are **a simple but powerful goal-setting framework**.

The first part is the **Objective**, which describes the goal.

The second part, the **Key Results**, describes our measures of success in making progress toward our goal.

These two pieces work together to form a simple, straightforward, easy-to-communicate statement.

Objectives

Objectives are the goals you set. The job of an objective is to inspire the team and provide a clear *why*. A good objective is inspirational, aspirational, qualitative, timeboxed, and specific. It connects people to the broader purpose of the work and is specific enough to create urgency. It's the reason we get out of bed and come to work every day. And, in our opinion, it's a significant opportunity to describe the benefit your work will generate for your customers.

Here's an example of an objective for a flying car company:

> *Redefine local and regional air travel in North America to make it simpler, safer, and more accessible by the end of this decade.*

This is a big objective, describing the ambition of an entire company. But OKRs work at a smaller scale, too. For example, if you work in the marketing department of this company, your department's objective might be something like this:

> *Create broad awareness of the safety and sustainability promise of modern flying cars by the end of this year.*

Objectives can express a goal at any level, from whole organization to department to big team to small workgroup. The higher up in an organization you are, the broader, more long-term, and more strategically focused your objectives will be. The smaller your workgroup, the more narrowly defined your goals will be.

Key Results

Key results are the way you measure progress toward your goal. If objectives seem lofty (and they should), then key results are what ground them. They give you specific, measurable criteria that let you know if and when you've met your goals and allow you to judge your progress along the way. They answer the question, *How do we know we've achieved our goal?*

For the flying car company's objective: *Redefine local and regional air travel in North America to make it simpler, safer, and more accessible by the end of this decade,* the key results might be:

- Deposit-paying customers sell out the waitlist for the first three model-year releases.

- Our operators cause no safety incidents during the first year of market rollout.
- At least 35% of local and regional travelers, both air- and land-based, are now regularly using our flying vehicles.

These key results, taken together, tell us a story: If we do all of these things, then we will achieve our objective. They also give us things to measure along the way. Is there demand for our products before they go to market? Can we deliver on our safety promise? Are local and regional travelers warming to flying cars?

Good key results measure value, and the best way to understand value is by measuring *what people are doing, or doing differently, as a result of our work.*

In this case, our key results tell us exactly what behaviors we're looking for: prospective buyers showing intent to buy the vehicle, operators learning to use the vehicles safely, and travelers shifting their choice of transportation toward our flying vehicles.

Or, as the book title says, "**Who does what by how much.**"

What do OKRs leave out?

There's an important thing that many goal-setting frameworks have that OKRs *don't* contain: **solutions**. This is by design. OKRs don't explicitly tell you how to achieve your goals. They're not task lists or instructions for how to succeed. They're not documents with requirements, specifications, or lists of features. What makes OKRs powerful is that they define a problem—*We want to win. Here's what winning looks like*—but they end up asking the people doing the work to *figure out* what to do: to use their expertise, initiative, reasoning, and creativity to solve problems. Working with OKRs grounds us in solving problems rather than simply implementing solutions.

We'll detail how to create great OKRs in Part 2 of this book.

Focus on Customer Behavior

We've said that OKRs help you focus on delivering value to your customers, but what does this really mean?

It means that OKRs change the way you measure success. A typical idea of success might be to measure whether an important task was completed. For example, *Did we launch that new flying vehicle on time?* With OKRs, though, we're looking at whether or not we *created value* by completing that task. We do that by looking at customer behavior. When we created our flying vehicle, did it create value for the customer? And how can we tell?

We can tell by paying attention to what our customers are doing, and doing differently, as a result of our work. Did we change customer behavior for the better? Did they show interest in the flying vehicle? Did they buy the flying vehicle? Did they start traveling more frequently in a flying vehicle? Did those things create value for them and for us?

Everyone Has a Customer

Right about now, you might be thinking, *This is all fine,* **but I don't have a customer.** You might work in a big company in a role that isn't very close to the end customer.

This was precisely the objection raised when we started working with Monica and her team at the shoe company. Stuart, the head of design there, said to us, "Guys, this makes a lot of sense for our e-commerce team, but I'm a *shoe designer.* Customers are buying the finished shoes, not my drawings or models of the shoe *designs,*" he said. "So, how do OKRs work for me? Whose behavior am I changing?"

This is an important question faced by just about everyone who starts using OKRs. Stuart makes designs for shoes. When he's done with a new design, he gives it to the brand manager, and from there, it goes to the manufacturer. During this process, many people will work with the design to figure out the details of making the shoe: materials, amounts, costs, etc. Marketing gets involved, too, thinking about how to create campaigns for the shoe.

Think about the people in this description: the brand manager, the manufacturer, and the people on the marketing team.

We asked Stuart: "Think about your work. How could you help your colleagues be more effective in their work? What could you change or do differently? The way you present the design? Your timing? The medium in which you deliver it?"

Think about this question for yourself. Who are your colleagues? What do they need from you? What do you need from them? How might you change the way you work to make everyone more effective?

"Oh, I see," Stuart said, nodding. "My work influences my *colleagues'* behaviors. *They're* my customers."

Exactly.

You might work with end customers, but you might not. Either way, you'll be making things in your job—shoe designs, vacation policies, or fundraising campaigns—and you make these things *for* someone. That person consumes it, which makes them *your customer*. Therefore, you influence their behavior, and your goal is to influence that behavior in a positive way: a way that benefits them by helping them be more successful and in a way that benefits you at the same time by creating value for your organization.

Who Does What by How Much?

OKRs are a goal-setting framework that embraces this idea because they describe success in terms of outcomes: valuable customer behavior.

Let's look at Stuart's OKRs to see how this works.

As we talked to Stuart, we came to understand that he was spending a lot of time making physical models of his shoe designs. These models were great, but they took a long time to make, and whenever there was a change, Stuart had to go through the time-consuming process of making new models. The whole process meant that the feedback cycle was long and slow.

So Stuart's OKR looked something like this:

Objective:
> *Make it easier for all necessary departments to*
> *provide design feedback by the end of the quarter.*

Key Result 1:
> *Brand managers (who) provide feedback (does what)*
> *50% faster on each shoe design (by how much).*

Key Result 2:
> *The manufacturer (who) produces physical*
> *prototypes of each shoe design (does what)*
> *100% faster (by how much).*

These key results are what we call "outcomes." An outcome is a *change in behavior that creates value.* Each outcome statement has three parts.

> **Who?** *Whose behavior are we talking about?*
> **Does what?** *What behavior are we talking about?*
> **By how much?** *What is the specific numerical target that we're talking about?*

This phrase is so important that we've used it as the name of the book. OKRs are all about distilling your goal-setting work down to this essential set of simple questions. This simple-but-powerful way of thinking about your work has the power to do amazing things.

OKRs Are a Process

OKRs aren't just a different way of talking about and writing your goals; they're also a different way of working toward them. Of course, it's essential to talk about your goals and to write your goals in a way that's clear and concrete. But if that's all you do, you won't reap most of the value OKRs promise. For that, you have to put them into use.

What does it mean to put OKRs into use? **At the most basic level, it means that we use them on a daily, weekly, monthly, quarterly, and annual basis to decide what to work on.** (Of course, there's a lot more to it than that, but we'll get into all that in a bit.)

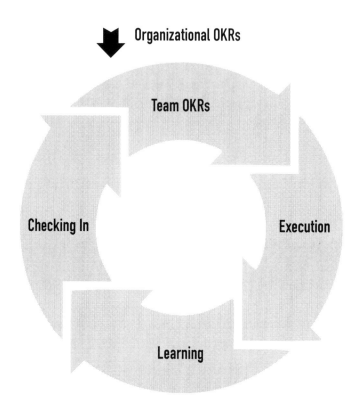

Most organizations that work with OKRs have implemented a version of **the OKR Cycle.** This cycle defines the activities that go along with using OKRs, from strategy-setting and OKR-writing to the regular rhythm of meetings that organizations use to review progress.

We'll cover the OKR Cycle in more detail in Part 3 of the book. For now, the important thing to understand is that we're not simply writing goals in a new way. We're using those goals continuously to guide our work.

OKRs Are a Culture

If you look at organizations that use OKRs well, you'll notice two closely related things. The first is that **each of these companies does OKRs a little differently from the next.** They've adapted them to the unique needs of their organization and industry. In other words, OKRs can and should reflect the specific culture of the organization using them.

As OKR expert Brett Knowles told us: "Rule #1 of OKRs is that there is no Rule #1." By this, he means that OKRs are a flexible and customizable framework. To use them successfully in your organization, you'll need to make them your own.

As a reader of this book, then, you'll have to navigate this question constantly. We're going to make many recommendations in the following chapters. We're confident in our recommendations because we've seen them work. But you'll come across ideas that may not make sense to you. Here's what we ask: Think critically about what we're telling you. If you're unsure about something, give it the benefit of the doubt and try it. But be willing to throw away our advice, too. Ultimately, OKRs work when you and your organization can make them your own. We encourage you to do that.

This brings us to the second thing that you notice when you look at organizations that use OKRs well: **Successful OKRs are deeply embedded in the organizations' culture.** Leadership champions them. Departments and teams adopt them widely and enthusiastically. The organization uses them as a critical management tool that guides what they do and how they do it.

They say *culture is what you do*. OKRs are a powerful tool for creating culture because they are all about changing what people do. We'll talk about ways you can make OKRs a part of your culture in Part 4 of this book.

For now, we hope it's enough to encourage you to think about how you can use OKRs to change what *you* do. When everyone in the organization does that together and with the same intention, amazing things can happen.

Key Takeaways

1. OKRs are a goal-setting framework that defines and measures success by achieving specific outcomes instead of by completing tasks or creating work product. Those outcomes are changes in customer behavior.

2. Everyone has a customer. Whether you provide a tangible product or an intangible service, the person who benefits from your work is your customer.

3. Objectives are the qualitative expression of an organization's or team's strategy in the form of specific and time-bound goals. They should inspire and align teams or organizations and provide a strong *why* for their work.

4. Key results are your outcomes: the changes in customer behavior you aim to see as a result of your work. These metrics tell you when you've succeeded in achieving your goal.

5. OKRs are not just a goal-setting framework. They're also a process. The OKR Cycle is the process of using OKRs to guide your work and steer it toward achieving your goals.

6. OKRs are also a culture. They work when they become deeply embedded in an organization's way of being and working.

Chapter 2

Why Use OKRs?

You may already know why you want to use OKRs. Perhaps you've read about the success that other organizations have had with them. Maybe you're trying to improve something at your company. Or perhaps you're reading this book because your organization decided to do OKRs, and you don't really have a choice. No matter where you're starting from, it's helpful to understand why OKRs are a powerful tool. That's what we're going to cover in this chapter.

One note before we start, though. Changing the way you work— whether as an individual, a team, a department, or an entire company— is hard. It takes time. In larger organizations, it can take years. It usually takes a lot of trial and error before you get it right. That's OK. When things feel difficult, it helps to connect back to the *why. Why are we trying to change the way we work? What's the benefit?* Remembering your answers to these questions can help you find new ways to navigate and overcome the obstacles that you face.

In that spirit, here are some reasons *why* organizations use OKRs and why you might want to use them, too.

The Benefits of Using OKRs

Work today requires us all to solve new problems quickly and often in the face of tremendous uncertainty and complexity. The tools that have emerged to deal with this moment are ones that allow us to be **agile** in our approach. What do we mean when we use this (admittedly often-abused) word? We're talking about lightweight ways of working that...

- Help us to be **customer-centric**
- Allow us to change course in response to **learning**
- Create **transparency**
- Grant people the **autonomy** to figure things out
- Provide the **alignment** and **focus** that organizations need to manage complexity.

OKRs do all of these things. They are incredibly well-suited to helping companies face the challenges of working today.

Now, let's look a little more closely at each of these ideas.

OKRs put customer value at the center.

Delivering value to the customer is the most critical factor for an organization's success. Whether you're a company selling products, a hospital system providing care, a government agency serving constituents, or a nonprofit advocating on an important issue, ultimately, you are trying to deliver value to someone. Everything starts there.

Why? Because delivering value to your customers will, ideally, make them happy. And if your customers—people who pay you for your product or colleagues who use the work you do—are happy with your products and services, if they find them to be useful and additive to their lives, they will come back for more and spread the word, thereby increasing your success. So, it makes sense that leaders and teams would want to prioritize making and doing things that create customer value.

It makes sense...and yet, too many still don't do that. It's easy to get caught up in the busyness of the day-to-day, working on tasks that we *assume* will provide value and never pausing to check if we actually did. Too often, we don't stop to observe, measure, and get feedback from our customers themselves. In fact, many traditional goal-setting frameworks encourage this by allowing teams to set task-centric or project-centric goals. The problem is that if you measure success simply as completing your to-do lists, you don't really know if you've *actually* created value for anyone.

OKRs, however, if you use them in the way that we describe in this book, build customer-centricity into your goal-setting process. You set objectives that spell out the improvement you hope to see in the customer's world. You learn how to measure success by setting key results that track the value you deliver to those customers—even if, like Stuart, the shoe designer, you think your work doesn't touch customers. It does! Everyone has a customer!

Admittedly, sometimes you'll see implementations of OKRs that don't put customer value at the center. We think that's a missed opportunity. Customer-centricity is at the heart of our approach to OKRs. That's one of the things that differentiates our approach from other ways of using the framework.

How Tesco turned from task lists to customer value

When setting out with OKRs, many teams face the challenge of figuring out where to start. You can start with internal needs—or you can start with customers.

We spoke with Daniel Booth, product director for the retail platform at Tesco, one of the world's largest supermarket retailers. Booth and his team have been working with OKRs for the better part of a decade. When it comes to online grocery shopping, there are so many places a team could start, so we wanted to know how Tesco decides what their teams should focus on.

Endless lists of requests

Booth shared that, like most organizations, Tesco teams don't lack for executive requests—their leaders regularly send lists of "stuff to make" to the technology teams. Before OKRs, the process of choosing which items from these lists to work on often involved circuitous discussions. These discussions usually got resolved by the highest-paid person in the room.

Booth thought there had to be a way to reframe these conversations. Tesco has tons of data on what their customers are doing in the virtual and physical stores. Booth decided to use that data, in the context of OKRs, to work through the long lists of executive demands.

Identifying and baselining friction points

Booth's team, the online retail platform team, has direct access to Tesco's customers and, therefore, is able to take advantage of fast feedback loops. Whatever they deliver has a direct impact on how customers shop, and they can see that impact in the data they get through their platform. This made the platform team the perfect candidate for getting OKRs off the ground at Tesco.

> Next, Booth started reframing the discussion with his stake-holders. He wanted to understand their goals in terms of the value they were trying to achieve rather than the features that they wanted built. These conversations helped them move from "When are you building the shopping basket improvements?" to "How can we increase average order value?"
>
> Once he had a sense of what the executives were trying to achieve, Booth started the process of creating OKRs to capture these goals. The team used analytics, research, and customer discovery work to document specific points in the shopping process that caused problems for shoppers. Then, they measured these friction points to understand the size of the problem and to correlate them to the goals that their leaders cared about.
>
> Booth's team used these baseline measurements as the basis from which they set their OKRs. The goal was always to improve over the baselines and then directly show the broader organizational impact of these tactical behavior changes.

This is what we mean when we say that OKRs can be customer-centric: Instead of looking inward at the company's wish lists, Booth and his colleagues looked *outward* toward customers. By understanding the obstacles customers faced and demonstrating how these obstacles impacted the company, Booth and his team were able to shift their focus, change the conversations, and ultimately deliver massive value to both customers and the company.

OKRs emphasize learning and autonomy.

OKRs are based on a radical idea: **Leaders should lay out their objectives, and the people in the organization should pursue those objectives.** When Peter Drucker first expressed this idea in the 1950s, it was a pretty radical departure from the conventional wisdom of the day, which held that bosses told workers what to do and workers did what the bosses said. It was the bosses "solving" problems. Drucker's idea for management-by-objective, by contrast, was to give workers a problem to solve and the means to solve it—but not the solutions. OKRs are built on top of this idea. They are, essentially, a way of expressing work as a problem to solve rather than a set of orders to execute.

And that's the interesting thing: **OKRs don't tell people what to do.** People have to figure it out. This means that working with OKRs gives people the autonomy to learn their way forward, to ask—and then answer—key questions. Do we understand the objective? Do we understand what we need to do to solve it? Do we know what the solution is, or are there ideas we need to test first? How do we know that our solution is working? Could there be other ways to solve the problem? OKRs provide a system that's all about answering these kinds of questions.

Incredibly, what was radical in the 1950s is still radical today. In most organizations, bosses and managers still tell workers what to do, decisions are still made based on the HIPPO (the highest income paid person's opinion), and everyone else still gets in line. After all, the boss has the power, and the boss got there for a reason, right? Sure—but remember: The boss' opinion is still *just an opinion*. It's not automatically right. Opinions and ideas are all hypotheses; they have to be proven true.

OKRs bypass the HIPPO problem. They framework a problem to solve and require us to measure our work to see if we're making progress and solving the problem. If an idea doesn't work—even if it's the boss' idea—the data will tell us. We try it, learn, and move on. It's just another idea.

OKRs use measurement and data to create transparency.

Leaders often feel cut off from what is happening in their organizations. Teams can get stuck in silos, lacking information and then working at cross-purposes. Even teams that work closely together can misunderstand one another because they lack critical information.

Everyone in an organization benefits from increased clarity about what's going on and how their work fits into the bigger picture. OKRs provide this.

OKRs drive transparency because they make everyone's goals clear. And importantly, they prompt conversations about what customers are doing and why they're doing it. Finally, they make it possible to have conversations about progress because they encourage measurement.

As we've said, OKRs require that you describe success in terms of measurable key results. That implies that when you use OKRs, you're measuring things.

The benefits of measurement are numerous, and they should be clear and obvious. Here are just a few:

- Measurement allows us to have better conversations about our work.
- Measurement allows us to assess whether or not our work is on track.
- It allows us to share our success.
- It allows us to talk objectively about our progress and the challenges we face.

Still, measurement creates challenges. First and foremost, you have to measure things! How do you do that? **Well, you need data.**

Sometimes, you have this data. Every organization tracks financial data. These days, many organizations also track customer behavior data. That said, it's often the case that the data we need to measure our progress is hard to get. Maybe that's because the systems we have for data collection are hard to use or they're managed by a different part of the organization. Maybe our organization doesn't collect that data at all. Or maybe the thing that we're interested in is hard to measure. These are real obstacles, and we'll talk about how to overcome them in Chapter 5. Still, the fact that it can be hard to find the data that you need shouldn't discourage you. In fact, one of the benefits of OKRs is that they put pressure on organizations, teams, and people to improve both their data collection practices and the access to that data within the organization.

One important thing to remember is that **data comes in many shapes and sizes**. We often think of data as hard numbers that live in a spreadsheet or on a graph, but that's only one kind of data. When we talk to our customers, those conversations are filled with data. Researchers call that "qualitative data." When we observe our colleagues at work, we're gathering data.

OKRs anchor teams' goals to a larger why.

To be engaged at work, teams need to feel connected to the purpose of their work. Yet, traditional goal-setting frameworks often focus exclusively on breaking down work into small units—typically, task lists—which also tends to break the connection between the work and the why. How can you feel connected to a larger purpose if you're simply handed a task list?

OKRs have the why built in. The whole point of the objective in OKRs is to organize the work around the purpose. What's more, because the culture of OKRs encourages sharing your OKRs with other teams, you can see what the rest of the organization is working on *and why they're working on it.* The why gets transmitted throughout the organization.

Finally, OKRs are set with a mix of top-down and bottom-up processes. You're not simply *handed* an OKR—or at least, you shouldn't be. Individuals and teams participate in the goal-setting process and then have the autonomy to make decisions about their day-to-day work. This allows people to bring their own intrinsic motivations to the work and increases their connection to the why.

OKRs create alignment and focus.

When was the last time that you looked at your to-do list and thought, "Gee. I really don't have enough stuff to do..." If your answer is "never," then you're in good company. Most of us face an overwhelming list of things that we could be working on at any given moment. In some ways, the most important decision we make each day is the choice of what to (and what *not* to) work on.

OKRs express an organization's most important goals and the strategy for pursuing those goals. They make clear what people should be working on and what they should save for another time. When organizations adopt and share them widely across all teams, OKRs facilitate the alignment that organizations desperately need to succeed.

OKRs provide focus. When distractions and new opportunities arise (and they always do), OKRs also give everyone a tool to prioritize and make choices. Should we stay on course with our OKR? Do we need to change our plans? Should we set aside this idea for another day? OKRs provide a structure to have these conversations. They help us make the best possible choices about how to spend our time.

OKRs work for every organization and every role.

There are many business frameworks created solely for tech companies, or solely for nonprofits, or solely for leadership. Similarly, there are many ways of working that work only for certain kinds of work—like software development or industrial production. Adapting those frameworks for work in other industries or roles can be challenging—and sometimes even useless. You can learn the framework, sure, but when you try to use it, you realize that the concepts don't apply to you, or they don't translate into the work of the team you have to collaborate with.

Stuart, the shoe designer, assumed using OKRs would be repeating that pattern. *I don't work directly with our customers, so this must apply only to the customer-facing teams in the company,* he thought. But, as Stuart learned, that's not the case. Nothing in OKRs is exclusive to any field, team, or industry because the framework focuses *everyone's* work entirely on *their* customers (whoever those customers are) and how to adapt their ways of working to serve them.

OKRs in the cement and ceramics industry? Yep.

OKRs got their start in the tech world, but they're being used today by companies in every sector of the economy. Grupo Industrial Graiman (GIG) is a 60-year-old ceramics and cement company based in Ecuador that employs nearly 1,200 people. GIG is definitely not in the tech world, yet the company use OKRs to great success.

In fact, as Andres Vinueza, the company's transformation manager, shared with us, GIG uses OKRs throughout the entire organization, from the president on down. And though shifting to a culture focused on outcomes has been challenging, OKRs have paved the way for the increased agility GIG needs to survive and thrive in an industry facing major change.

"Natural gas keeps us in business"

Along with many other industries, the world of ceramics is shifting toward using sustainable energy sources. However, the ovens that GIG uses to make their product cannot function on electricity alone; they require natural gas. This presented GIG with a problem: Natural gas contracts are often driven by a country's government. The government's pace didn't align with GIG's needs. They couldn't wait for the Ecuadorian government to secure continuous sources of gas for their use, so the company took the matter of finding more sustainable sources of energy into their own hands.

Traditionally, GIG would have approached this challenge with a to-do-list approach: *Contract with the government for reliable natural gas delivery.* In this case, though, they used OKRs to express the goal in a new way. The company created an objective to become a more sustainable company in the near future; GIG's key result was to secure two new, sustainable sources of natural gas in the next year.

Experimenting to find the best energy provider

Vinueza told us that though looking for nearby providers made a lot of sense, GIG's key results inspired the company to experiment with different approaches than in the past, which meant looking at processes and producers further afield. In one experiment, GIG collaborated with a German natural gas producer to test the possibility of introducing hydrogen into their ceramic tile production.

Ceramic tile production at scale is a complicated process involving rare raw materials, high temperatures, and large machinery. It's also a centuries-old industry with standard ways of operating, which makes it difficult for companies to move away from "the way we've always done it."

GIG is bucking convention and using OKRs to help innovate. Building new relationships with a variety of suppliers enables the company to make their partners, themselves, and Ecuador more prosperous and sustainable. GIG's ongoing work proves that, at its heart, the OKR framework can spur innovation and new ways of working in nearly any industry—even one based on centuries of tradition, rare materials, and industrial machinery.

Principles for Using OKRs

There are no ways of working that work in every situation. Every tool, technique, and framework needs to be adapted to make it work in a given situation. Think about it: Imagine using the same way of working in a giant hospital system, in the government, in a tech unicorn, and in a chain of mattress stores. Absurd, right?

And yet, OKRs are used in all of these places. How can that be? Well, it's possible because OKRs are flexible, and many very smart people have found ways to adapt them to their needs.

We want you to do that, too. We recognize that there's no single right way to use OKRs, and we want you to make them your own.

We do, however, have many opinions about what works and what doesn't. (That's the point of this book!) So although we believe in the "rules" that we're going to share with you for using OKRs, we also want you to make OKRs your own. In that spirit, we want to offer these principles that you can use to guide your use of OKRs.

If you find yourself having trouble with OKRs, we encourage you to come back to this section and review these principles. For example, one important principle of OKRs is **focus**. If you're having trouble, ask yourself, "Are we using OKRs in a way that helps us focus?" If the answer is "no," then consider changing the way you're using OKRs to help you and your organization create more focus.

Here, then, are the key principles of OKRs:

1. Focus
2. Autonomy
3. Alignment
4. Accountability
5. Transparency
6. Agility
7. Customer-centricity

The Key Principles of OKRs

1. Focus
No team can work on everything all at once. OKRs answer the question, "What have we agreed to work on together?" and, by extension, "What have we decided is not a priority?" In doing so, OKRs provide teams and organizations with a clear focus for their work through which every question and decision gets filtered.

> *Anti-pattern:*
> *People try to express **all of their work** as an OKR, which results in too many OKRs and unclear prioritization. Real focus means fewer OKRs.*
>
> *Solution:*
> *Use OKRs only for the current strategic priorities. Everything else either fits under a "business as usual" umbrella or waits for the strategic priority to focus on it.*

2. Autonomy
Individual teams are the closest to the work and, thus, are in the best position to judge how to create value in their area of responsibility. OKRs acknowledge this by giving teams the responsibility of writing their OKRs and then creating the results.

> *Anti-pattern:*
> *Leaders define OKRs for the whole organization without the input of the teams themselves. This is top-down governance that allows for no collaboration and grants no actual autonomy.*
>
> *Solution:*
> *Teams set their own goals, linking each goal to a higher-level goal.*

3. Alignment

Alignment and autonomy are two halves of the same coin. Teams using OKRs need to coordinate to ensure everyone—both the people on their individual team and everyone on adjacent teams—is rowing in the same direction. Aligned, autonomous teams allow an organization to actually focus on its stated goals.

> **Anti-pattern:**
> *Teams working on similar projects silo themselves, focusing only on their individual team's goals and limiting coordination with adjacent teams. They become "cowboy" teams that choose their own direction regardless of what others are doing around them.*
>
> **Solution:**
> *Teams working on similar projects share an OKR, uniting and focusing their efforts while driving intrateam transparency. All teams can link their OKRs to "parent OKRs" at a higher level in the organization.*

4. Accountability

There's a third side to this coin[1], though: accountability. One of the reasons that organizations limit the autonomy of their teams is the fear that teams lack the responsibility to operate independently. OKRs give organizations a powerful tool for accountability. They let teams declare their goals and then monitor and measure their progress. They make this visible to their peers, leaders, and the rest of the organization in ways that promote this accountability.

---

1   OK, we know there's no such thing as a three-sided coin, but autonomy, alignment, and accountability are so tightly connected that we're sticking with this metaphor.

Anti-pattern:

> Teams operate without concern for business results,
> focusing (sometimes in well-intentioned ways) on
> tasks that don't create value for the organization.

Solution:

> Teams use OKRs to set their goals transparently,
> working with peers and leadership to ensure these
> goals align with organizational goals. Then, teams
> use the OKR process to hold themselves accountable
> and to communicate their progress with the rest of
> the organization.

5. Transparency

To maintain alignment, teams need to constantly share progress with one another and their leaders. That requires a high level of transparency from everyone involved at all times.

Anti-pattern:

> When teams don't share their progress consistently,
> or aren't used to doing so, they can default to
> limited communication, which causes duplicate
> efforts, conflicting or competing work, and an
> overall lack of alignment across teams.

Solution:

> OKR work and progress are shared publicly and
> broadly in a central system anyone in the company
> can see.

6. Agility

Agile means many things to many people. For us, though, the most basic idea of agility is *the ability to change course in response to learning.*[2]

---

2   For our readers who work in tech, we're talking about agility with a lower-
    case "a," not Agile. The quality, not the cult.

OKRs help teams be more agile. You work in short cycles to solve the problem at hand, track your progress, and pivot as needed based on the evidence received from your customers. You measure success in terms of the value you create for your customer.

> **Anti-pattern:**
> *Teams use OKRs in a set-it-and-forget-it fashion. They don't check in often enough, and/or they don't have permission to make changes based on what they learn from customer feedback.*
>
> **Solution:**
> *Teams check in on a weekly, monthly, quarterly, and annual basis to ensure goals and work are aligned with strategic and market priorities.*

7. Customer-centricity

OKRs provide a way to focus on work that makes a real difference by creating outcomes—customers doing something differently in a way that's valuable. To do this, your work has to focus specifically on your customers—even if your customer is an office colleague who consumes the product of your work. Focus on making them successful and you'll be successful too.

> **Anti-pattern:**
> *Teams write OKRs that focus on making stuff. Remember: Stuff isn't valuable unless it creates a positive outcome.*
>
> **Solution:**
> *Teams write OKRs where both the objective and the key results are based on a better state for the customer as visible through their behavior.*

Each of the key principles above are things many leaders strive to cultivate in their organizations and among their teams. They're also things that make your work, as team members, much better, easier, and more successful on the whole. When you're using OKRs to the fullest extent, these are the principles that will both drive your work and shore it up.

Key Takeaways

1. OKRs keep your customers—internal, external, and beyond—front and center in all of your conversations and work.
2. OKRs increase organizational agility, making it easier to respond to changes in the market more quickly.
3. OKRs drive transparency among teams, aligning them more effectively and reducing duplicate effort and waste.

Chapter 3

OKRs and Outcomes

How do you define success in your work? How does your organization define success?

We often define success as the completion of a task or the launch of a product or initiative. When we think about it that way, it's easy to say we've accomplished something. After all, we've finished it. We've crossed it off of our to-do list. But does launching a product or ticking off a box always lead to success?

It does not.

In this book, we're going to use a very different definition of success. **Success means that you've created a valuable outcome.**

This chapter is all about that idea. We'll talk about what we mean when we say "outcomes" and why outcomes are so important for OKRs. We'll also define a few other important ideas that will help you succeed with OKRs.

By how much?

Who?

A measureable change in customer behavior that creates value

Does what?

What Do We Mean by Outcomes?

Let's start with the definition of "outcome": **An outcome is a measurable change in your customer's behavior that creates value.**[3]

There's a simpler way to say this, though: **Who does what by how much?**

- **Who?** This is the person, or customer, we're thinking about.
- **Does what?** This is the valuable behavior we're trying to create.
- **By how much?** This is the *measurable* part—where we specify our target for the behavior change.

In other words, an outcome is when a person—our customer—does something valuable that we can observe and measure in some way. Let's look at a couple of examples.

Google Glass

Think about some of the biggest failed tech products of the last 20 years. It would be hard to leave Google Glass off that list. Launched in June 2013 with great fanfare, Google Glass promised to deliver sci-fi functionality to every smartphone owner. Essentially a tricked-out pair of eyeglasses, they were loaded with tech: a small, transparent display screen attached to their upper right corner, a hidden camera, speakers, a microphone for making video and audio calls, and Wi-Fi and Bluetooth connectivity for internet use. You were supposed to be able to manage your calendar, answer text messages, Google the recipe you planned to make for dinner, and call your mom—all without having to take out, or even look at,

---

3   We recognize that this is an opinionated definition that's a little different from some other familiar definitions of the word "outcomes." We've found that this definition, because of its specificity, transforms the idea of outcomes from a somewhat vague concept into a very practical management tool. For a deeper dive into the idea of outcomes, we recommend Josh's book *Outcomes Over Output*.

your phone. The glasses were the company's first big push into wearable technology—a then-nascent market—and early news of the product caused a big splash.

They were a massive failure. Why? No one wanted to use Google Glass. People thought they were awkward, cumbersome, and ugly. So even though they were an arguably amazing technological achievement, they failed because making cool technology is not enough to succeed. To succeed, they needed to produce an outcome—a change in customer behavior that creates value. For Google Glass, the fundamental behavior change was simple: People buy and then wear the product. Well, the product failed on both fronts. People didn't buy them, and they definitely didn't wear them.

Unlimited Vacation

Most companies in the United States have historically given employees a fixed number of vacation days a year—typically just 10 days. However, sometime in the early 2000s, certain tech companies started to notice that employees weren't using all their vacation days, and as a result, they were burning out. So, these companies began experimenting with unlimited vacation policies, allowing employees to take as many vacation days as they wished, as long as they got their jobs done. It seemed ingenious. After all, who wouldn't take more vacation if it was available?

Turns out, many people wouldn't. These unlimited vacation policies failed. When companies offered people unlimited vacation, people actually *took less vacation*—a result that has continued to bear out as more companies have adopted unlimited vacation policies in the decades since. One theory as to why this happens is that employees worry that if they take more vacation than their colleagues, they'll be considered less hard-working or that it'll hurt their careers. Another theory blames the companies for not normalizing the idea that people should take vacations. Whatever the reason, these policies didn't create the desired outcome: They didn't get people to take more vacation. Instead, they had the opposite effect: less vacation and more burnout.

What's the connection between unlimited vacation and Google Glass? In both cases, you can see the difference between *making stuff* (vacation policies, fancy glasses) and *creating value* (less burnout, whatever people were supposed to do with those glasses). We call the stuff that you make "output," and, as we've said, the value that results "outcome."

Let's look at both of these words in more detail.

OKRs and Outcomes

Outcomes are important, because in our way of thinking, you need to express your key results as outcomes for OKRs to be successful.[4] To understand the significance of outcomes, though, we also need to understand the terms "outputs" and "impact."

Logic Model

We first learned about these terms[5] from a framework called the Logic Model, depicted in the diagram below. The core idea of this model is that we make outputs, which hopefully create outcomes. Ultimately, we hope that the outcomes contribute to our long-term goals. We call those long-term goals "impact."

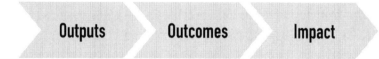

Output

The stories about Google Glass and the unlimited vacation policy have a key thing in common: The people involved *made something.* Google made a product called Google Glass. Various companies' HR departments made unlimited vacation policies. These things they made were

---

4   Remember: There are no absolutes in the world of OKRs, but this rule is one that you need to have a very, very, very good reason to break.

5   We've adapted these ideas from the work on Logic Models developed at the W.K Kellogg Foundation. See the Resources section at the back of this book to learn more.

their "output." Output can be products, policies, laws, promotions, content, advertisements—really anything made by humans.

In both stories, we can evaluate the success of the output not just in terms of technical fitness but also in terms of the value it provided (or didn't). Google Glass "worked" on a functional level—it was actually something of a technical marvel—and we can imagine that the vacation policies were "technical" successes: legal, legible, logical, and clear.

And this "technical" success *is* important. When we make stuff, we want it to be good. For instance, we want our cars to operate safely and not burst into flames. We want our ads to be written well and easy to understand. But "working" in this sense is the bare minimum. It's table stakes. We need stuff to do more than simply "work" if we want to create value.

The problem with Google Glass and unlimited vacation policies wasn't that they weren't functional or easily understood; it was that the output didn't change people's behavior in a way that created value. In other words, the output didn't create the *outcome* that the companies wanted.

This is why we don't use output as a key result. Just because you make something doesn't mean that you've created value. Imagine, for example, these two different key results:

> **Option 1: An output-based key result:**
> *Manufacture 100,000 Google Glass units for public release by Q3 2013.*

> **Option 2: An outcome-based key result:**
> *10,000 people purchase and become active users of Google Glass by Q4 2013.*

Which one of these is a better measure of value creation? Sure, it's a big accomplishment to design, build, and ship Google Glass. Lots of people did a lot of good work to make that happen. But did all that work create value? It did not.

Outcome

We've already discussed outcomes a bit, so this one should be easy: An outcome is the measurable change in human behavior that we see when people receive our output. In other words, outcomes are the measures of success (or failure) of our output. **These are your key results.**

For example, "We created Google Glass" is not an outcome; it's an output. An outcome, or key result, that would signal success from that output might be "25% of Google Glass customers use the product every day."[6]

Outcomes tell us, empirically, when we've delivered something of value (or not)—whether or not we've solved a problem for our customers or improved their experience. If our expected outcomes aren't met, we missed something with our output—perhaps a mistake in the business model, poor feature placement, a chaotic rollout, inadequate marketing, etc.

To find an outcome, ask, "What will people be doing differently when we give them our output?"

Impact

Impact is the high-level, long-term measure of success. For businesses, these are things like revenue, profit margin, market share, customer satisfaction, and churn. For nonprofits, they tend to be mission-driven: things like increasing human lifespan or happiness, eradicating disease, etc. As you'll see in future chapters, we'll sometimes (but very rarely) use impacts when we write our objectives. We avoid them when we're writing key results, though, because in almost every case, impacts are too big—and the result of too many factors—to be able to work on them directly. (We'll look at this in more detail in Chapter 6.)

---

6   You'll notice that we try to always use the format [who] + [does what] + [by how much] when we write outputs/key results. The actual order of these phrases doesn't matter. What matters is that you have all three as part of the statement and that the statement makes sense.

What About KPIs?

Whenever we work with companies on OKRs, someone will ask us about KPIs. "Where do KPIs come into play?" they say.

KPI, which stands for "Key Performance Indicator," is a phrase you hear frequently in the corporate world. It refers to a metric or calculation that the company uses to measure the health of the business. The problem is "KPI" is a fuzzy term. Anything can be a KPI! There isn't a standard set of KPIs, nor any agreement about what makes something a KPI. In other words, there's no true definition of what makes something a KPI other than that someone's decided that it's "key."

So KPIs are important by definition, and they can show up in many places when we use OKRs. If your organization has KPIs, use them as conversation starters. You want to understand how your OKRs relate to your KPIs. Can you make a connection between your OKR and one or more KPIs? Is the logic clear?

But trust us when we say, there's no definitive one-to-one mapping between a KPI and any part of the OKR framework.

How They Work Together

When you're identifying measures of success and setting OKRs, every one of these things—output, outcomes, and impact—comes into play.

- Leadership identifies the high-level **impact** they want to see and the strategy to achieve that. They express these ideas as high-level, organizational OKRs.
- Leadership communicates the organizational OKRs to all teams.
- Teams create their OKRs by identifying key results they need to achieve and expressing those key results as **outcomes**.
- Teams share their OKRs with leadership, tying them back to the company goals.

- Then, teams figure out and deliver the
  output to achieve those outcomes.

What does this look like in practice?

Imagine that you work for an organization that is committed to being a great place to work.[7] The organization places so much value on this goal that it has created an organizational OKR around it.

> *Objective:*
>> *Be the best place to work in our industry within one year.*

The key results for this objective are...

> *Key Result 1:*
>> *Increase the number of employees who would recommend us as a place to work by 10% compared to last year.*
>
> *Key Result 2:*
>> *Reduce regrettable turnover by 10%.*

Notice that these key results are outcomes: people doing things that are valuable. Here's how Key Result 1 breaks down according to our "Who does what by how much?" framework:

> **Who?**
> *Employees*
> **Does what?**
> *Recommend the organization as a place to work*

---

7   This is a real OKR, which we've borrowed from the Cleveland Clinic. The rest of this story in this section, however, is fictionalized. https:// my.clevelandclinic.org/-/scassets/files/org/about/who-we-are/ state-of-the-clinic?la=en

By how much?
At a 10% higher rate than last year

Now, imagine that you work in the HR department and you're thinking about that second key result: regrettable turnover. You might have data that says that people leave their jobs when they're burned out and that one way to reduce burnout is to get people to take their vacations.

Working with your team then, you might create your team's objective for the year:

Objective:
> Create a sustainable work environment that
> responds to changing employee needs.

One of your key results might be:

Key Result:
> All employees take two to three weeks of
> vacation each year.

You and your team are excited by this prospect, and you believe that if you can just change the company vacation policy, you will achieve your goal. You believe that one way to do that might be enacting an unlimited vacation policy.

If we were to lay this out as a visual model, it might look like this:

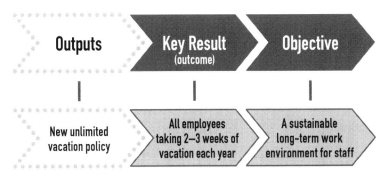

Why do you need all these stages? Well, let's imagine that we don't yet know that unlimited vacation policies don't work. So, you have written and committed to an OKR, and now you can try many different things to try to achieve our goals. A new unlimited vacation policy is one possible tactic, but there are other things that you can try, too. You might shut down the company for a few weeks and force everyone to take a vacation. You might make managers responsible for creating vacation schedules at the start of the year. You might make people take off a minimum number of days each quarter. Whatever ideas you come up with, the point is that, with OKRs, you can test many ideas and measure the outcomes of those ideas to see which ones work best.

OKRs allow us to frame our goals in clear, actionable ways, and they give us the yardstick that we can use to measure our progress.

In this case, let's say that you decide to try the unlimited vacation policy. You might create a test group, then look at their vacation data over the first few quarters of the year and compare that to last year. Is the new policy working? If it is, great. If not, you might consider a pivot. Your work is no longer just about making new policies; it's now about achieving outcomes. And how do you know that you've achieved your outcomes? Well, remember that outcomes should fit the question "Who does what by how much?" *Does what* is key.

To understand outcomes, we need to watch what people do.

Customer Value Creates Business Value

"Value" is one of the most ambiguous words in business. It means different things to different people, and people at various levels of an organization love to throw it around without clarifying what it really means. Executives talk about providing "business value." Customer-facing teams highlight providing "customer value." And internally facing teams like human resources and cybersecurity will say "organizational value." It's possible to break down each of these ideas in greater detail, but we don't need to. For our purposes and yours, **creating business value, customer value, or organizational value is all the same**.

Look at it this way: If you create things that...

A. Make your customers successful,
B. Respect their time,
C. Solve real problems for them in meaningful ways, and
D. Are a delight to use...

Your customers will reward you with...

a. Business,
b. Loyalty, and
c. Word-of-mouth marketing and promotion.

It's the same logic if you work on an internally facing team and your customers are your colleagues: If you create things that make your colleagues more successful, respect their time, solve their problems in meaningful ways, and are a delight to use, you will make them more efficient, effective, communicative, and collaborative—all of which lead to better results for the end customers and the business on the whole.

Essentially, the actions our customers take—whoever our customers are—as a result of our products and services determine if our business will be successful. Seen this way, defining value becomes clear: **If we're making our customers more successful, we're delivering value. Value for them is success for us.**

Once an organization speaks about value in the same terms—from top to bottom, at all levels of the company—many other things fall in line, including incentives, prioritization, and decision-making. We break free of a world in which people cite "value" without truly pursuing it. And there's no confusion or attempt to divide efforts between serving the customer *or* the business because those two aims are one and the same.

Because OKRs put the focus on achieving behavior-driven outcomes instead of on completing tasks or making specific products, you learn right away how to identify and target the customer behaviors that indicate what's valuable. And since providing customer value drives business results, by extension, OKRs also help you understand how to prioritize your work and that of your team—regardless of seniority level—according to what activities and efforts will drive the most value the fastest.

Key Takeaways

1. **Output** is the stuff we make or do to generate an outcome, whether that's producing something, providing a service, or implementing a policy. **Outcomes** are the observable, measurable changes in human behavior that result. **Key results** are outcomes because actions without desired results will not achieve your objective's success.

2. **"Who does what by how much?"** is a simple way to frame your outcomes and ensure they focus on the right things. "Who" is the person, or customer, you're thinking about. "Does what" is the valuable behavior you're trying to create. "By how much" is the measure of behavior change you're targeting to be successful.

3. **Impact** is a measure of high-level and long-term organizational goals. An organization's objectives are often aimed at creating greater impact, but impact is too high-level for teams to focus on because you can't measure day-to-day progress according to high-level metrics. Teams must focus on tactical key results instead.

4. Prioritizing output and task completion doesn't tell you whether or not your efforts will be successful with your customers and improve business results. Instead, organizations need to prioritize providing their customers with value. Value to the customer equals value to the organization.

Part 2

Writing OKRs

Now it's time to write your OKRs. This part of the book is your step-by-step instruction manual for that process.

We'll talk about strategy and how it is the basis for your OKRs, especially at the organizational level. Then, we'll guide you step-by-step through writing OKRs for your company and then for your teams. We'll talk about how writing OKRs is a collaborative process that encourages both top-down and bottom-up communication. Finally, we'll answer the most common questions that we've heard about OKRs over the years.

Chapter 4

Strategy and OKRs

A client we worked with this year asked us to come in and help them establish OKRs for their entire product development organization—nearly 1,500 people. We were thrilled. This was an opportunity to help the organization move from its traditional output-focused management techniques to a more modern outcome-focused approach. This would be a critical transition for the company: An influx of startups was eroding their market share, and their market-leading position was under serious threat. They felt an urgency to adopt new ways of working.

As we sat down for one of our first meetings, we asked, "What's the company's strategy for the next year?" The question was met with blank stares and an awkward silence. This was a dead giveaway that something was wrong. Either they didn't have a strategy, or they didn't know what it was. "Isn't that what OKRs do?" they asked us.

If only this was a unique conversation. Many organizations believe that rethinking their goal-setting framework will somehow magically deliver the right strategy. This is understandable. A lot of the conversation surrounding OKRs is about how to write good OKRs. That's important, of course, but just as (or more!) important is writing **the right** OKRs.

You can write OKRs—even well-structured ones—but still focus on the wrong stuff. So how can you ensure that, given all of the things you *could* focus on, you're focusing on the right stuff? That's where strategy comes in.

When OKRs work, it's because they are helping your organization focus on the right stuff. In other words, **OKRs work when they reflect and express your strategy.** So in this chapter, we'll give you a useful and straightforward way to think about strategy, and we'll outline a simple process that you can use to create your strategy.

What Is Strategy?

Now, most people think of strategy—at least in the business world—as the realm of the C-suite and of highly paid management consultants. In other words, they see it as a tool for steering the whole organization. Though strategy certainly has an important place there, we believe that strategy is for everyone.

To understand why we say that, let's start with our definition of strategy: **Strategy is an opinionated and coherent approach to addressing an important challenge.** In other words, it identifies a challenge and defines how to deal with it.

So why do we say that strategy is for everyone? One reason is that important challenges are everywhere.

Think about your work and your team. How should you approach that work? Let's say you are facing an important deadline. What's the best way to rally your team in order to hit that deadline? Your answer... that's a deadline strategy. Or let's say that you've just taken a new role in a new company. How are you going to make a great first impression? Your answer...that's your onboarding strategy.

Think about your personal life. How do you stay healthy? That's your wellness strategy. How do you raise your kids? That's your parenting strategy.

So even though we don't often use the explicit tools of strategy, every critical challenge that we face in any realm of our lives can benefit from the tools of strategy.

Strategy and OKRs

If you're setting OKRs for your team, then you're using strategy, whether you know it or not. You're making decisions about your important challenge (that's part of your objective), and you're making implicit decisions about how you'll approach your goal when you write key results that express what success looks like.

So, you *can* create OKRs without an explicit strategy, but it's much harder if you do it that way. That's why we recommend starting the OKR process with a short discussion about your strategy. In the second half of this chapter, we're going to share a set of simple, practical questions that we use as a tool to help teams discuss and decide on a strategy. These questions work at the team level, the department level, and even the organizational level. You can even use them in your personal life. The key is that they are fast and lightweight.

But before we create a strategy, it's useful to look a little more closely at exactly what we mean by "strategy."

A Closer Look at "Strategy"

We said earlier that strategy is *an opinionated and coherent approach to addressing an important challenge.* Let's look at each part of this definition.

> **Strategy addresses an important challenge.**
> *Important challenges are ones that don't have obvious or easy solutions. (If the solutions were obvious or easy, we wouldn't need strategies; we'd just solve the problems.) At any given moment, the world is full of important challenges. When you select a challenge to work on, you're making the first important decision of strategy: Where should we focus? Why should we work on this one instead of that one?*

This question, "Which challenge should we address?" goes to the heart of why strategy and OKRs are so tightly related, and why it's so important to think about strategy when creating your OKRs. Without a strategy, how will your team know where to focus their OKR energy? How will you select your objective? Why would you select *this* objective as opposed to *that* objective?

Strategy is opinionated.
Strategy involves choices. It's about what you're choosing to do and how you're choosing to do it. Equally important is what you're choosing not to do. Let's say that you're trying to lose weight. How are you going to do that? What are you not going to do? If you're trying to lose five pounds to look good at an event that's in a few weeks, you might choose a crash diet. But if you're trying to maintain a healthy weight for the rest of your life, you'd probably avoid crash diets in favor of a more sustainable approach. The point here is not so much that one choice is right and one is wrong; it's that you're making a choice between viable alternatives, based on what you need at the moment. And you do have to make a choice. Otherwise, you're not following a strategy— you're simply reacting.

Strategy is coherent.
The various parts of your strategy must play well together and must reinforce one another. For example, let's say your strategy is to create a luxury brand that sells watches. You want to create a brand that stands the test of time. To do that, you'd probably set your prices quite high, but you also need your quality to be high. If you simply charge a lot of money but produce a cheap product to save costs, you won't end up with a sustainable business.

To be clear, either of these elements could be part of a successful strategy. You could produce cheap, disposable goods and charge a low price for them. That would make you a low-cost brand. You could produce expensive goods and charge a premium. That would make you a premium brand. These are different strategies, but both could work.

What you can't do is create a cheap brand selling expensive products or an expensive brand selling cheap goods. Either of those strategies would be incoherent and unworkable.

In practice, the way this shows up for most of us is that we need to make sure that the strategies we create for our teams are aligned with the larger organizational strategy. Do you work for an organization with a luxury brand? You'd want to think carefully about strategies for your team that might contradict that. Do you work at a low-cost brand? You'd probably avoid premium suppliers. The point here is to understand the larger strategy and then use that as your starting point.

> **Strategy is an approach.**
> *Strategy isn't a plan; it's an approach. What do we mean by that? Well, a plan might be something like, "I'm going to work out three times a week." Plans are good—but also fragile. You can plan to work out three times a week, but what happens when you get busy with work, get sick, or miss a day because your car breaks down and you can't get to the gym? To deal with those circumstances, you need a policy as well. You can think of policies as guidelines, rules, or guiding principles. They help you make decisions when unexpected things happen. Your policy might be something like, "When I miss a workout, I forgive myself and stay on schedule." Or a different policy might be, "When I miss a workout, I make it up the next day." A good strategy is a mix of policy and plan.*

How to Create a Strategy: A Lightweight Process

There are many frameworks out there for strategy. Most of them help you solve strategy problems in a certain context (e.g., marketing strategy, product strategy, positioning strategy, etc.). The process that we're going to describe, though, is fairly generic. It's a useful way to approach strategy in many contexts.

As with most of the methods we share, we consider this a lightweight approach. You should be able to sit down with your team and, in the space of a single workshop, emerge with a credible first draft of your strategy. This doesn't mean that spending more time won't be valuable; it simply means that we believe that this framework can create a lot of value and clarity for you with just a small amount of time invested.

Here's an overview of the process:

1. **Identify your biggest challenge.**
   Strategy exists to guide us as we address important challenges. So what's the big one that you're facing?
2. **Determine where you will play.**[8]
   To address your challenge, which people, markets, geographic locations, etc., will you focus your energy on?
3. **Propose how you will win.**
   What mix of policy and action[9] will you deploy to address your challenge? What will your winning approach be?

---

8   We're indebted to Roger Martin's work on strategy. We've adapted these key questions from his book, *Playing To Win.* Martin, Roger L., and A.G. Lafley. *Playing to Win: How Strategy Really Works.* Harvard Business Review Press, 2013.

9   The idea that strategy is "a coherent mix of policy and action designed to address an important challenge" comes from Richard Rumelt's book *Good Strategy Bad Strategy: The Difference and Why It Matters.* Crown Business, 2011.

Let's look at each of these steps in more detail.

1. Identify your biggest challenge.

Your first step is to identify the most important challenge that you face. Depending on your role, you can look at this on two levels: the organization-wide level and the team level.

At the Organization-wide Level

If you're in a leadership position, you're thinking about how to make the whole organization successful. What's your goal? What are the obstacles in the market that your organization must overcome to achieve that goal? What challenges do you face?

For example, a few years ago, we worked with a tech startup in a then-crowded field: machine-learning process automation. If this sounds complex, that's because it is. The company was working on a powerful tool to help large corporations automate important and repetitive tasks. The problem they faced was that it took a long time to install, configure, and train the software before customers got any value from the product. This meant that our client had a number of interested companies who had started slow-moving pilot projects, but none had converted to long-term paying customers.

As we spoke with the client's executive team, we discussed the various dimensions of this problem. Was it a problem of differentiating themselves from the competition? Was it a problem of managing operational costs? Could they make their capital last until they had a real customer win? After much conversation, the CEO finally stood up and said, "Look, our problem is *time to value.* It takes us too long to deliver value. We have to focus everything we have in the next six months on creating rapid value for our customers!"

The executive team agreed: *Time to value* would be the major challenge that they would focus on for the coming year.

This was an important moment for that team. They'd been arguing all morning, and they welcomed the clarity and strength of the CEO's opinion. More importantly, they agreed with the logic. It was compelling:

Their long pilots were expensive and demoralizing, and they didn't convert customers. They believed that if they could deliver value sooner, they'd see more sales.

Coming to an agreement on the problem they most needed to tackle put the executive team in a position to write their organization-wide OKRs, which they would then roll out to the teams, who in turn would create their own OKRs.

One thing that's important to emphasize here is that finding your most important challenge is a simple thing to describe, but it's hard to do. Even in the story above, you can see a room of smart, engaged, and capable executives struggling to find clarity during the process. So though it may be simple, it's not necessarily easy. In later chapters, we'll talk about how adopting an experimental mindset can help. For now, just remember that you're going to need to make a decision—and then be prepared to test your decision early and often to see if you got it right.

At the Team Level

If you work at the team level, you're going to be thinking about how your team can contribute to the organization's goals. You have to ask, "What is the organization trying to achieve, and what work can this team do to advance or support those goals?"

Your first step is to look at the organizational goals. Do you know what they are? Is there something you can start with? Is there a company strategy or a set of company OKRs? If so, you're in very good shape.

Working from Organizational Goals

With your team, consider the organizational goals. How does your team's work fit into the broader organizational context? What is the most impactful thing that your team can do to support your organization's strategy? Is there some problem or obstacle that your team can unlock? In other words, what is your most important challenge?

For example, consider the company we just described. They decided to focus on "time to value." If you were working there, how might your team contribute to that? If you're on a tech team, you might think about technology solutions. But if you're on a marketing team, you might be thinking about how you could start telling this story to the marketplace. A sales team might go looking for new clients that respond well to the idea of "faster time to value." A security team might think about what procedures and processes they have in place that either slow things down or, conversely, speed things up. And an R&D team might go looking for innovative approaches to speed up value delivery.

Whatever area you work in, you want to look at the intersection of your team's responsibilities and your organization's goals and then think creatively about what your most impactful contribution could be. To be clear, you always want to be able to make a clear connection between your team's strategy and the larger organizational strategy.

It's important to note that team-level challenges don't live in a vacuum. In the same way that you want to consider organization-wide goals, you also want to consider the work that your peers are doing. Are there important initiatives elsewhere in the organization that are depending on your work? Are you dependent on another team? Conversations with these groups can often reveal larger challenges—ones that make sense to collaborate on, which might even result in a shared strategy and shared OKRs for the teams involved.

When you've selected your most significant challenge, you're ready to move to the next step in the process: defining your approach to solving your challenge.

2. Identify your market.

To determine how to approach your important challenge, start by looking at your market. As Roger Martin says in his book, *Playing To Win*: "Where will you play?"

Who are the people that you're going to focus on? Where will you find them? What do they value? How do you position or categorize your product, service, or company in order to fit within an existing market or define a new market?

If you work at the organization level, think about the market(s) that your organization services. If you work at the team level, then you *might* think about your external customers or even a subset of those customers, but you might think about *internal customers* instead.

For example, the leadership at the automation company we've been talking about might ask, "Which external customer segment is likely to get the most value most quickly from our product?" Internal teams would think more specifically about their targets. A marketing team might focus on journalists or influential industry bloggers, for example, whereas a tech team might think about building tools to make their customer-facing sales engineers more effective.

When you've defined the group of people that will be the focus of your approach, you're ready to move to the next step.

3. Propose your unique competitive approach.

Now you've got two important building blocks. You know the challenge you're facing and the market that you want to focus on. Now, we're going to look at what you need to do to win. What's your unique, competitive approach to addressing this challenge? What are the things that you need to do? What guiding principles will you use to make decisions along the way?

Here are some more useful questions to consider when defining your strategy:

- What value will we deliver to our market?
- How will we capture value from the market?
- How does this address our biggest challenge?
- What is the differentiator that our competitor can't or doesn't want to match?
- How might we leverage an existing or unique asset of ours?
- How does this support the larger organizational strategy?

Your answers here should tell a logical story. They should be short and simple—you should be able to summarize them on an index card or tell the whole story in an elevator ride. This last part—storytelling—is critical. Your strategy—from challenge to market to approach—must make for a compelling story.

Internal Teams Have Competitors, Too

When we talk about strategy, we often talk about identifying your unique, competitive approach in relation to other organizations in your market. How does Toyota compete against Ford, for example? But how do you identify a unique, competitive approach if you're an internal team? Who is your competitor then?

For internal teams, one way to think about competition is to consider what people in your organization currently use to solve the problem. Maybe you want people to use an official vacation request form on the company website to submit vacation requests, but the form is too clunky, so people just send emails to their managers instead. In this case, your "competition" is email. Or maybe you want people to use the new expense reporting system you've put in place, but people hate that system and keep submitting requests on the old Excel template. In this case, your "competition" is Excel.

For internal projects, it can be useful to think of these things as competitors, because then you can ask useful questions like, "How can we be better than our competitor?" Or, "How can we make our vacation request system better than submitting requests by email?" Or, "How can we make our expense system better than Excel?"

Storytelling: Make the Logic Visible

Once you have created your strategy, you want to share it with your stakeholders. The best method that we know for this is storytelling. In fact, the first test your strategy faces is whether or not it makes a clear and compelling story.

Here's an example from a time Jeff worked at an online recruiting company.

Let's go back in time and imagine that you work at this online recruiting company, too. The company operates a website that places highly skilled executives in highly selective and well-paying jobs. To do that, it serves job-seekers, recruiters, and companies offering exclusively high-paying, full-time jobs.

One morning, the CEO sends an email to the entire company that reads:

> *"We're abandoning our years-long strategy of only*
> *offering full-time jobs and are moving into hourly and*
> *part-time job offers."*

After reading this email, you would likely immediately wonder, "Why?" (Maybe your first thought wouldn't be expressed quite this politely.) After all, you've been working on this service for years. You understand the users. You understand the market. Now, all of a sudden, you're being asked to do something completely different and new. You'll do the work, of course, and you'll do your best to change focus to this new target audience and value proposition, but you probably have many questions. "What's the vision? How can I align with my teammates and leaders about the new direction? What do I do when I face the many unknown situations that this new market will present?"

All this feels... Well, trust us when we say that it's not a good feeling.

Now, imagine instead the CEO had sent a different email—one that captured the strategy in a clear and compelling story:

"Over the past five years, the number of full-time job opportunities available in our market has steadily decreased. At the same time, inbound inquiries from both employers and job-seekers looking to fill part-time roles has grown 35% year over year. This is a market opportunity we can no longer ignore. Offering hourly and part-time roles on our site has the potential to raise our annual revenue by 47% in the first 12 months alone.

"Starting next week, we are going to reassign some teams to begin supporting this new market. We remain dedicated to our original mission. However, as market conditions evolve, we must continually reassess how to best spend our time."

This is a very different email. It makes a clear, compelling case for the new strategy. There's a challenge (the decreasing size of the existing market) and the approach to solving it (going after a promising, adjacent market). It's a short, clear story, and one that will be easy to retell.

Don't underestimate that last point: **Telling compelling stories about the organization's goals and your teams' work is part of your job.** A big part, in fact.

As a leader, you need your teams to care—about their work and that of the organization. For them to care, you need to help them understand the logic behind what you want them to do. They need transparency. Good storytelling accomplishes all of these things. Every time you communicate with your colleagues, you have an opportunity to tell a compelling story that makes the logic of your decisions visible in a way that's meaningful to them and provides clarity. Sharing your strategy is one of those key opportunities.

Key Takeaways

1. **Strategy** is an opinionated and coherent approach to addressing an important challenge. In other words, it identifies and challenge and states the approach that we'll use to deal with that challenge.
2. **Strategy is for everyone.** We often associate strategy with the C-Suite, and the highest levels of an organization. But anyone can be strategic and use the tools of strategy, because important challenges are everywhere.
3. **Without Strategy, OKRs will fail.** OKRs are a tool for expressing strategy. They describe the most important things that you need to focus on, and they describe how you'll approach that work. Without strategy, you won't have a clear picture of what these things are, which can make OKRs an exercise in going nowhere.

Chapter 5

Who Does What?

It's our strong belief that OKRs work best when they are built around people. This means that we use people-centric measures of success—outcomes—as our key results. Remember Chapter 3? We said that an outcome is *a change in human behavior that creates value* and that you can always define an outcome using the formula [*who*] + [*does what*] + [*by how much*]. **Well, this chapter is about figuring out your outcomes: your [who] + [does what].**

To do that, we'll consider three questions:

1. **What does your team have control over?**
   More than likely, your team's work doesn't (and can't) touch every part of the business, so your OKRs should focus only on what you can control and change. Which elements of the business, product, or service does your work involve? Those elements are your scope of control.
2. **Which customers will you target first?**
   With this question, we'll look within your scope of control to determine which people your team will focus on.

3. **What behaviors from this target audience drive business results? Are there parts of the customer journey keeping your customers from exhibiting those behaviors?** Finally, we'll use a simple storytelling technique to reveal the critical behaviors that you want to target in your key results.

Defining Your Important Outcomes

What Does Your Team Have Control Over?

If you work on a marketing team, you wouldn't focus your goals on security policy, right? You'd leave that to the security team. That seems obvious, but it points to something important that we often miss in OKRs: We spend too much time thinking about the big, organization-wide goals and not enough time narrowing our focus to the things we can really control. So, our first step here is to orient our work specifically to our roles and responsibilities. Ultimately, which pieces of the puzzle fall within our team's scope?

One thing that can make OKRs difficult is when teams don't have the autonomy to pursue their goals but are instead dependent on other teams to make progress. In the long run, it's generally better to evolve your team structure to reduce dependencies and increase team autonomy. In the near term, however, you need to deal with the current reality. If you find yourself in a situation in which your progress is tightly tied to another team or set of teams, work with these teams to coordinate your OKRs. You might choose to operate from a single, overarching OKR, or you might choose to use complementary OKRs. Either way, you need to figure out a way to move forward together.

This is a good moment to consider your team's strategy, which we talked about in Chapter 4. What's your biggest challenge? Is working on that challenge within your scope of control? If it is, great. If not, you're going to need to make some adjustments—either by picking a different challenge, narrowing which part of that challenge you want to address, or perhaps broadening (carefully) your team to include the people you need to work on this challenge.

Who: Which Customer Will You Target First?

Let's spend a little time now thinking about that second question: **Who?**

Getting Specific

When you're thinking about putting people at the center of your work, it helps to be as specific as possible. For example, imagine that you work at a sneaker company, and the company is thinking about making a new shoe. You might start by thinking about who was going to buy the shoe. These days, just about everyone owns a pair of sneakers, so you might say that you're designing a shoe for everyone. After all, you want everyone to buy it, right? The problem here is that if you design a shoe for everyone, it probably won't be a very good shoe. It's true that our grandparents wear Nikes, and so does Michael Jordan, and so does that cute little toddler next door who is just taking his first steps. But they're not wearing the exact same Nikes, are they? These people clearly have different needs, so it stands to reason that if we design shoes that suit each of their needs— instead of "everyone's"—we'll make better shoes.

It's possible to take this logic too far, of course. We could focus with laser-precision on one person's needs, but if a large number of people don't share these needs, then we're probably being too focused. Grandpa Frank liked to keep a $20 bill in his shoe. Does that mean we should build miniature billfolds into every shoe? Unless there are a whole lot of Grandpa Franks out there, probably not.

You want to be specific about the customers you should target *and* make sure those customers make up a full, viable group.

With all this in mind, let's move on to our next step: figuring out **who will be the focus of our work**.

External Customers

Consider your team's scope of control. Who are the people that directly consume your work? You and your team might do work that faces external customers. Let's keep going with the sneaker example and say that your company makes athletic shoes, specifically. Maybe you work on the marketing team, and your strategic focus this year is on youth sports.

Considering the different people in this market, you may think about the kids in youth sports, the parents, or the coaches. Or maybe you're focusing on a different part of the business—buyers for big retailers or influencers in the market, like celebrities, online influencers, journalists, or celebrity stylists.

Note that not all of these people are "customers" in the strict sense of the word. They may not be the people who buy your shoes, but they are all likely critical in the purchase process, which makes them important for your success.

There's probably an area of focus in the external market that is both important to you and related to your scope of control. If this is the case for your team, you're going to want to select your "who" from this group.

Internal Customers

Not everyone does work that is directly consumed by external customers. You might work in a more internal-facing part of your organization, like analytics or human resources. When this is the case, you want to consider a couple of questions:

> **Is there something you work on that can help make the people who DO work with customers more effective?**
> *For example, maybe the people who work with customers need better data. If you're on a data team, whoever needs better data to do their jobs better are your customers. This might even be the people on the marketing team that we just described above.*

> **Is there something that you work on that makes the entire organization more effective?**
> *Maybe you work in the facilities department, and you're responsible for keeping the company offices in great shape. Or maybe you work in HR, and you've got responsibilities for the well-being of company employees. You'd find your customers in these "markets."*

Create a list of potential "whos" to focus on.

1. **Make a list of the different people and roles in your market.**
   You can do this work by yourself or brainstorm the list with your team.

2. **Aim for somewhere between three and six plausible roles in your market.**
   You don't have to decide which group of people are going to be the focus yet. At this point, it's more important to just create a small set of candidates.

Does What?

Once you've assembled a list of the people you might want to focus on, it's time to figure out what behaviors you're going to focus on—the "**does what**" part of the equation.

Telling a Story

At this point, we can start to break things down by telling a story about our customer and their journey with our product or service. These stories are simple but powerful ways to discover important success metrics. Here's an example. Let's say that you, like us, have long fantasized about starting a business selling donuts. We don't want to compete with any of the big chain stores—at least, not in the beginning. We want to start small, with just a small operation, and test our idea. So, let's tell a story about our ideal donut buyer.

Our ideal donut buyer is a young person on their way to work who wants a little treat to go with their coffee. They buy the donut when they get off the train on their walk to the office. Then, they go to the office, sit down at their desk, and enjoy their donut and coffee.

It's a simple story, but we can already start to draw out some success metrics from the story, and we can use those metrics to make some early decisions about our business.

Let's first pull out the behaviors:

1. Our customer takes the subway to work.
2. Our customer buys a donut and coffee after getting off the train.
3. Our customer carries the donut and coffee to their office.
4. Our customer eats the donut and drinks the coffee at work.

To be successful, then, we'd be looking for...

- A high number of people who take the subway to work: Foot traffic is a potentially important measure for us.
- People exiting the subway and walking to work: This is the *specific* kind of foot traffic that will help us.
- People who buy both a donut and coffee: This means that we need to sell both things, and we'll want to measure the percentage of people buying both, not just one or the other.
- People who don't eat the donut on-site: Our buyer takes it to work. This means we're going to optimize our business for takeout, and we'll want to measure whether we're right or wrong about this idea.

So, here are the measurements that we can nominate for potential key result targets:

- Foot traffic to our location (the number of potential donut buyers who pass our location each day)
- The number of people who buy both a donut and a coffee
- The number of people who order to-go versus those who eat their donut on-site

Plot the Customer's Journey

This process—telling a simple story, examining it for the important steps, then using these steps to create measures—is the basic process that we use to find outcomes. The outcomes that we find here will be important for us: We're going to use them as the basis of our key results in the next part of the process.

The process of describing and documenting your customer's journey can be very simple (you just tell a story and pay attention to the important things that people do in the story) or it can be more involved. Designers and researchers use this technique extensively and have developed techniques to tell these stories in great detail. In that world, the process is called Customer Journey Mapping or User Story Mapping.[10] If you have designers in your organization, they can help you to tell these stories and document them. But if you don't, don't worry. Just follow the basic process that we describe here. Even a simple storytelling session will yield great results.

---

10   If you want to learn more about story mapping, we recommend Jeff Patton's excellent book, *User Story Mapping: Discover the Whole Story, Build the Right Product.* Patton, Jeff, with Peter Economy. *User Story Mapping: Discover the Whole Story, Build the Right Product.* O'Reilly Media, 2014.

Understand Your Customer's Journey

1. Tell your story about the person or people who are the focus of your work.

2. If you want, write your story out as you work, as in the diagram below.

3. Pay particular attention to what people are doing in the story.

4. Pull out somewhere between three to six important behaviors: things people do that are important, that create value, either for them, for you, or ideally, both.

5. Write down those important behaviors, using the [who] [does what] format.

Our donut shop story might look like this:

Donut Shop Customer Journey

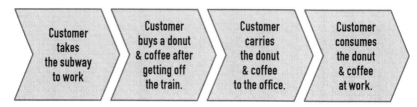

Once you have written down the important behaviors in your customer's story, you'll notice something important: If you've been careful and used the [who] [does what] format, then each box is a potentially important outcome.

These boxes, your potential outcomes, are what you'll use in your next step, when you're writing your OKRs. They'll form the basis of your key results.

Helpful Tips

As you're working through this exercise, here are some important tips to keep in mind:

Tip #1: Make sure every box is written in the [who] [does what] format.
This helps to ensure that each box contains a human behavior—which is the basis for your outcomes and key results. (We'll get to the "by how much" part in the next chapter.)

Tip #2:
Make sure your story focuses on steps within your scope of control.
There may be key steps in the customer's journey that are outside your scope of control. For example, in this donut shop story, "customer buys a donut" is an important step, and in our small operation, everyone contributes to this story. But if you work at a giant donut chain, say as a delivery driver, then "customer buys a donut" is definitely not within your scope of control. Your customers are the people who work in the stores, who have to use the ingredients that you deliver to make the donuts. So though "customer buys a donut" is still an important step (and you can include it in your story), it's not one that you control directly—so it's not a step or behavior that you should consider as a potential outcome for your key results.

Tip #3: Look for obstacles.
When you're telling your story, try to include both positive and negative factors. You're looking for things that contribute to success, but also the obstacles that contribute to failure. You can ask questions like, *What do people do to get through the story successfully?* Or, *What parts of the story are obstacles that get in people's way?*

Customer Journeys Aren't Always Clear

Sometimes, it's hard to have visibility into your specific customer's story. You might lack data, or you might be too far away from the customer. If you find yourself in this situation, we suggest these options:

1. Add a data scientist or analyst to the team. If you can, find someone who knows the numbers and ask them to join you for this exercise. This person should be able to not only access the data but also interpret it and identify patterns.

2. Add someone who knows the customer to your storytelling sessions. There are probably people you work with who can shed light on your customers in ways that you can't. Your salespeople or customer support people probably have some firsthand knowledge of your customers. You might also have people in departments like customer experience, user experience, market research, market insights, or user research. These people are experts in getting to know customers, and they can certainly contribute to this part of the process. Reach out and invite these folks in.

3. Guess. That's right. You know your product and your customer well enough to take a guess. You won't be 100% wrong. You likely won't be 100% right either, but guessing will at least give you a direction to explore. If you do find yourself having to make guesses, you should plan to prioritize discovery and fact-finding as one of the next steps in your process.

> We strongly recommend maintaining a bias toward action. Too many teams wait for data before doing this work. Don't wait. You know enough to take a guess and start experimenting. You'll be able to course-correct as soon as you need to.

Congratulations, You're Ready to Write Your OKRs

At this point, you've gathered all of the pieces that you need to write your OKRs.

- You've defined your **scope of control** and, if necessary, figured out **which teams you'll need to work closely with to create your OKRs**.
- You've created a list of people that you might want to focus on—your **"who" list**.
- You've walked the people on your who-list through one or more stories and used these stories to find **your outcomes**. You should have a list of potentially important outcomes to take into the next step.
- Got all these pieces? Great. Let's go write some OKRs.

Chapter 6

Writing OKRs

It's time to start writing your OKRs. This chapter is a step-by-step guide to doing that.

Generally, OKRs are best created in collaboration with your team, so gather your colleagues around a whiteboard (or a virtual whiteboard), bring the materials that you created in the last couple of chapters, and let's get to work.

Review: What Is an Objective?

The first part of your OKR is your objective. The point of the objective is to describe the goal that you are setting. The main job of an objective is to inspire the team and provide a clear *why* for the work. A good objective has four qualities:

1. **Inspirational:** It connects the team's work to a broader purpose. It should inspire people, help them connect to the meaning behind the work, and motivate them to pursue the goal.
2. **Qualitative:** It describes a strategic aspiration without quantifying it.
3. **Timeboxed:** It includes a deadline by which you believe you will achieve it (or by when you'd like to).

4. **Specific:** It focuses on a key element of your strategy instead of making a generalization.

Here's an example of an objective for a health-care company:

Become the market leader in the virtual mental health-care industry in North and South America by Q4 2024.

This is a big objective, describing the ambition of an entire company. But OKRs work at a smaller scale, too. For example, if you're in the marketing department, your unit's objective might be something like this:

Improve brand recognition in Latin America and Canada by the end of Q3 2024.

The idea here is that objectives can express a goal at any level, from whole organization to department to big team to small workgroup. Generally speaking, we want objectives to be as specific as possible, but the level of specificity will vary according to the size and responsibility of the team—in other words, according to the team's scope of control, an idea that we talked about in the last chapter. The higher up in an organization you are, the broader, more long-term, and more strategically focused your objectives will be. The smaller your workgroup, the more narrowly defined your goals will be.

As much as possible, try to have your objectives focus on the benefit you're trying to provide for your customers. Why are you pushing to increase brand awareness? Perhaps it could be because you want people to know they now have a new option to deal with a long-standing problem. As with the entire OKR process, always keep the customer in mind as you write your objectives.

Finally, it's important to note that this objective doesn't say *how* we'll succeed. It doesn't say, *build seven hospitals* or *acquire all of our competitors*. Solutions don't come until later in the process.

Focus on the Most Important Work

A common question that organizations face at the start of the OKR-writing process is *how many OKRs should we create?*

At the organizational level, you want to have a small set of OKRs—probably two or three—that represent different dimensions of your business. Or, if you're a big organization, you might want to have one OKR per business unit or other major division. Regardless, we think that when you're starting your OKR journey, less is more. Start with one and build from there.

At the team level, we recommend having only one OKR.

In both cases, we recommend setting two or three key results per objective.

Remember, one of the most important reasons to use OKRs in the first place is to create focus. You can't focus if you have too many focuses (or foci, if you want to be precise). Narrow things down by determining the most important problem you have to solve right now. You may have many problems, but you have only one most important problem. This is where you focus at this moment. It doesn't mean you ignore the other issues. It does mean you're not focused on them for now.

Creating Your Objective

To identify what your team's objective should be, take the following steps:

1. Gather what you need.

If you worked through Chapter 4 and Chapter 5, you have created the raw material that you'll need to create your OKRs. Specifically, you're going to want to have these things on hand:

- Your organization's strategy and your team's strategy
- Your team's most important obstacle
- Your organization's high-level OKRs
- Your scope of control
- A list of potential customers to focus on
- A list of potential outcomes that you might pursue

If you have these things, spend a few minutes getting familiar with them. (If not, you'll probably come to a moment in the process where you'll need to try to define these things. That's OK, just expect to have some additional conversation on these points.)

2. Identify your biggest obstacle.

Now, what's the biggest obstacle that stands between you and success?

You may have already identified this when you were working on your strategy. In Chapter 4, we called this your "important challenge." If you recall, in that chapter, we talked about an automation company that faced the challenge of delivering "faster time to value" with their product.

Here, you want to examine that challenge and identify the obstacles that you face in addressing that challenge.

If you're not sure what your challenges and obstacles are, here are some questions to consider.

At the organizational level: If you're writing OKRs for your organization, you want to think about how to make the whole company successful. What are the obstacles in the market that you need to overcome? What are the things standing between being the organization you are today and the organization that you want to become?

At the team level: If you're working at the team level, you want to think about how your team can contribute to the organization's goals. What is the organization trying to achieve? Do you know its high-level goals? Do you know what the company strategy is? Do you know the company OKRs?

Identify those things, then identify what work your team can do that will advance or support a part of that goal.

For example, your organization's strategy might be focused on improving the customer experience in the coming years. A high-level OKR that reflects this is:

Objective:
Provide the best customer experience in the industry within two years.

Key Result 1:
100% of new enterprise customers are fully onboarded and using our product within 30 days of signing their purchase contract.

Key Result 2:
Existing customers make referrals at a 25% higher rate than last year.

Key Result 3:
Customers who experience serious issues that require support become boosters, renewing their contracts at a 100% rate.

If you work in this organization, you might look at these key results and ask, "What's the biggest obstacle to achieving these results, and specifically, which of those obstacles fall within my team's responsibility?"

If you're on the support team, you might think about the biggest obstacle to providing world-class support. It might be that you're understaffed or your teams need training or you outsource support to a vendor that is cost-effective but not actually that good.

If you're on the operations team, you might look at this OKR and think about how much manual work the team needs to do to get new customers set up. It's almost impossible to get the customers set up in 30 days, much less get your own internal systems ready for those new customers to go live.

These are examples of the kinds of obstacles that you want to identify at this stage.

- *Working with these questions, create a short description (one or two sentences) of your biggest obstacle.*

For example, the team in the story above may write something like:

> *"It's impossible to get our customer set up quickly*
> *because setup requires a huge amount of manual work,*
> *both at the client's site and on our internal systems."*

3. Turn your obstacle into a positive statement.

To write your objective, take the big obstacle you identified and turn it into a positive statement. If you solve the problem, what does that look like? To be clear, we're not asking *how* we will solve the problem. Instead, we're trying to describe what the world looks like, or how it has changed once we've solved the problem. We'll be defining both "Why are we doing this work?" and "What do we hope to achieve, and by when?"

For example, the team in the story above might turn their obstacle into this positive statement:

> *"We can set up our customers quickly and easily because*
> *there is almost no manual or custom work involved for*
> *each customer."*

Now, we can use this positive statement as the basis for our objective. Remember, your objective statement should be:

- **Inspirational:** It connects the team's work to a broader purpose.
- **Qualitative:** It describes a strategic aspiration without quantifying it.
- **Timeboxed:** It sets a deadline by which you believe you will achieve it (or by when you'd like to).
- **Specific:** It focuses on a key element of your strategy instead of making a generalization.

To turn our positive statement into an objective, revise it so that it meets these four criteria. For example, we might revise our positive statement into this objective:

> *"To ensure our customer experience is the best in the world, by the end of the year, we'll be able to set up our customers quickly and easily because we won't need to perform manual or custom work for each customer. "*

Let's break down the pieces of this example:

- **Inspirational:** "To make sure our customer experience is best in the world" connects to the higher goal—the company strategy.
- **Qualitative:** "quickly and easily" are the qualities that we're looking for (remember, we'll measure this with our key results).
- **Timeboxed:** "by the end of the year" sets our time horizon.
- **Specific:** "won't need to perform manual or custom work" tells us the area of focus of this work.

Now, it's OK to write shorter objective statements. We've used many words here to illustrate the point, but we're OK with being more concise as long as you cover the important dimensions of the problem. Here are a few more examples, based on the story above.

- **Objective for the Customer Support Team:** The best customer support from the most knowledgeable and effective support staff in the industry by the end of the year.
- **Objective for the Product Development Team:** Create the most intuitive and easy-to-onboard product in the industry by the end of the year.

4. Self-Check your objective.

Review your objective. Make sure that it meets the following criteria:

- It's a positive statement.
- It's inspirational.
- It's qualitative.
- It's timeboxed.
- It's specific.
- It doesn't contain a solution.

A simple OKR process... Part 1

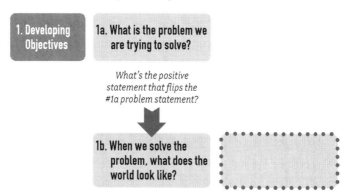

5. Find your parent.

One of the most important goals of the OKR process is to create alignment in the organization. We want people to focus their work on the right stuff, and we want everyone moving in the same direction. But if each team is writing its own OKRs, how do we do that?

By making sure that every OKR has a parent OKR and that all of the OKRs in the organization can, in some way, trace their purpose back to the overarching organizational OKRs. In a small organization, this is pretty easy to do. Each team could just look at one of the organizational OKRs and say, "our OKR is related to this OKR." In larger organizations, though, you may have many layers, business units, workgroups, etc.

There may be OKRs at every level. It's important in this case that there be some way to maintain alignment.

Note that it's not important to maintain a strict organizational hierarchy. In other words, a team should be able to choose *any* OKR as the parent of its OKR. What is important is that each team can tell a clear story about how its OKR supports the larger goals of the organization.

We'll talk more about this in Chapter 16.

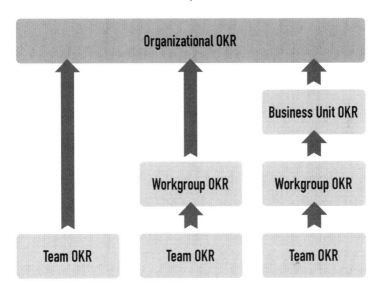

Review: What Are Key Results?

Key results are the way you measure progress toward your goal. If objectives seem lofty (and they should), then key results are what ground them. They give you the specific, measurable criteria to help you judge your progress and let you know if and when you've met your goals. They answer the question, "How do we know we've achieved our goal?"

Let's look at the key results in the example we've been using in this chapter. Here's that again:

Objective:
Provide the best customer experience in the industry within two years.

Key Result 1:
100% of new enterprise customers are fully onboarded and are using our product within 30 days of signing their purchase contract.

Key Result 2:
Existing customers make referrals at a 25% higher rate than last year.

Key Result 3:
Customers who experience serious issues that require support become boosters, renewing their contracts at a 100% rate.

These key results, taken together, tell us a story: If we do all of these things, then we will achieve our objective—to become the market leader. They also give us something to measure along the way. What is our rate of new customer growth? Are we retaining our existing customers? Are we growing our network?

There's another important thing we want you to notice in this example. These key results are **outcomes**. In other words, these key results are all *measurable changes in human behavior that create value*. Each key result contains the answer to all three questions: [who?] [does what?] [by how much?].

This last piece is what is going to make your OKRs customer-centric. Although your objective might not actually mention customers (though it's fine if it does), your key results need to.

Finally, it's important to reiterate that, similar to objectives, key results don't say *how* we'll succeed. They don't say, *Build seven hospitals* or *Acquire all of our competitors*. We'll save solutions for later in the process when we put our OKRs into motion. (See Part 3 for more on that.)

Creating Your Key Results

To create your key results:

1. **First, gather the important behaviors that you wrote down when you were telling your customer story.**
   This is the moment to refer back to your list of potential customers and the stories that you've created that describe their behavior. You'll find lots of raw material to work with in those stories.

Let's look at another objective from this company, this one from the support team:

> **Objective for the Customer Support Team:**
> *The best customer support from the most knowledgeable and effective support staff in the industry by the end of the year.*

So this team would look at the story of how customers receive support. They would tell this story and pull out the key steps of the story to use as the basis of their key results.

2. **Turn this into two to four statements that use the format of our titular question:**

   [who] + [does what] + [by how much]

   - The "who" needs to be a human—your customer.
   - "Does what" is the behavior you want to change in that human.
   - "By how much" is the measure by which that behavior needs to change (either increase or decrease) to achieve your objective.

This diagram walks through some key questions and steps to guide you:

A simple OKR process... Part 2

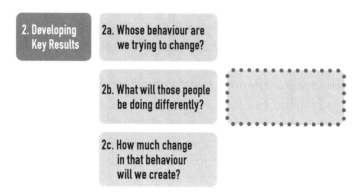

Key results for our support team above might look something like this:

Objective for the Customer Support Team:
The best customer support from the most knowledge-able and effective support staff in the industry by the end of the year.

Key Result 1:
Customers get the answers that they need through our online customer support channel instead of the call center at least 75% of the time.

Key Result 2:
Customers speak to fully trained customer support agents 100% of the time.

Key Result 3:
Customers who interact with customer support agents have their problem resolved on the first contact 95% of the time, and by the end of the second contact 99% of the time.

Self-Check Your Key Results

It's time to review your work.

1. **Make sure your key results are outcomes.** The easiest way to do this is to be strict about using the [who + does what + by how much] format.
2. **Make sure that your key results aren't solutions.** In other words, they shouldn't say *what* you're planning to do or to make. They should just describe the results of your work. Sometimes, people try to slip solutions into their key results by disguising them as human behaviors. For example, "We will design, build, and launch our new portal by the end of the year." Tricky, but wrong. Don't describe *your* behavior. Describe your customer's behavior.
3. **Make sure you can answer "yes" to the following question: If we achieve all of these key results, will we have achieved our objective?** If yes, congratulations! You've created a good set of key results for your team. If not, then take a look to see what you might be missing.

In the example above, our customer support team might achieve Key Result 1 (customers get answers online) and Key Result 2 (support staff is well-trained), but without also achieving Key Result 3 (customers getting their problems resolved), they will not have achieved their objective, which is to provide the best customer support.

Setting Your Numbers

Key results are far more actionable when they include specific numbers. Consider the difference between "Increase retention of weekly customers" and "Increase retention of weekly customers by 35%." The second key result gives the team clear direction; the first is merely a guiding principle.

One of the hardest parts of writing key results, however, is deciding what specific number to target. When we start working with numbers, there's an expectation that we can use math to figure out the *right* answer. The truth is a bit unsettling: There is actually *no* right answer.

Instead, it's more accurate to say that there are a range of answers, all imperfect, and you want to find an answer within that range. To do this, you'll need to have some conversations, use the data available to you—which will probably be imperfect—and make some smart guesses. In the end, you'll be able to come up with a *good* answer, not the right one.

So, how can we find that good answer?

A good numerical target should be based on two factors:

1. What's possible?
2. What's valuable?

What's Possible?

When we set OKRs, we want to be clear-sighted about what we can and can't do. Lots of the talk about OKRs concerns setting ambitious goals. That's great. Ambitious goals are possible. The Wright brothers built a flying machine! NASA sent humans to the moon! These are big, audacious goals, and some said they were impossible. But clearly, those folks were wrong. So, asking what's possible is an important part of goal-setting, as long as it's done in the right frame of mind.

What is possible, and how can we know in advance? Unfortunately, we can't. The only reason we know flying machines are possible is that the Wright brothers succeeded. Same with NASA sending people to the moon. Will it be possible to send humans to Mars? Only time will tell.

Sometimes you can predict what's possible with a high degree of certainty. You have data or precedent to look to. That's great. Say you want to sell a million pairs of shoes. You know that's possible because other companies have done that. What you don't know is if *your organization* can do that. Or if *these particular shoes* will prompt a million sales. In these cases, the question isn't exactly about the theoretical possibilities, but you're still sort of in the fortune-telling game.

Given that, knowing what's possible is often a guess. You need to look across the table at your team and at your stakeholders and have those hard conversations. We think there's a lot of value in these conversations, and we encourage you to embrace them.

What's Valuable?

The value question is a little easier to answer because we can usually quantify the result. If you sell 100 pairs of shoes, is that valuable? How about 10,000? 1,000,000? These numbers are easy to work with and can quickly tell you if an initiative is worth pursuing.

Still, these numbers can be subtle, especially when you're not working with sales or financial data. What if you're trying to make it easier for people to register on your website? If you increase registration rates by 1% is that valuable? What about 10%? What about 100%? Ultimately, you're going to need to build a model and have conversations with your team and your stakeholders.

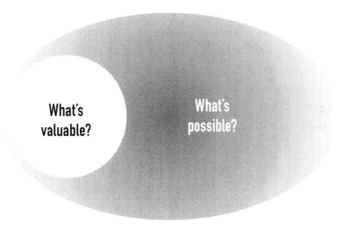

Aligning People Around Numbers

Have you ever tried to pick a place to eat with a large group of coworkers? Usually, the pre-lunch conversation goes something like this,

"Hey, where does everyone want to go for lunch today?"

"I don't know."

"No idea."

"Where do *you* want to go?"

Reacting to an open-ended question is hard, especially in the moment. Sometimes, it's better to give people a choice to respond to. Instead of asking folks where they want to go for lunch, ask them if they want to go to McDonald's. Without fail someone in the group will say, "Ew! I don't eat fast food. Why don't we go to this new vegetarian place that just opened up around the corner?"

Then someone else will say, "Vegetarian? Have you eaten at the place on 38th Street? It's amazing!"

And pretty soon, you've had a good conversation and settled on a place. It works every time.

Why are we talking about McDonald's and vegetarian restaurants? Because in the same way it can be difficult for a group of people to pick a lunch place, it can be tricky to get teams aligned around numbers. But giving people distinct options to start the conversation helps.

Instead of asking an open-ended question like, "What number should we assign to this KR?" ask "Is it worth it if we can increase our average order value (AOV) by 5%?"

All of a sudden, the team has something definitive to respond to. Someone might say, "Well, 5% is only about $2 per order, and even with 25,000 weekly customers, the cost of doing the work will exceed any benefits. We should try for at least a 15% increase in AOV."

Once the team is discussing actual numbers, you can have the value and feasibility conversations we mentioned above.

What's the Score?

Many teams (and consultants) advocate for "scoring" your OKRs. We're not particularly enthusiastic about scoring OKRs, but it can be a useful tool, especially at this stage, when you're trying to define your key results.

Let's talk about what scoring means and why we don't love it.

Scoring is the process of giving a grade to your performance. For example, let's say that your OKR is to increase foot traffic to your retail store by 100% this quarter. At the end of the quarter, you've grown foot traffic but only by 50%. Is that good? Is that bad? Should you continue to work on that OKR? Should you revise it? Should you abandon it?

Teams use scoring to help answer these questions. To score their work, they define a grading system at the same time that they define their OKRs. For example, they might say that growing foot traffic by 100% is an A, 80 to 99% is a B, 50 to 79% is a C, and anything under 50% is a failure. (Some teams use numerical grades; others use red, yellow, and green.) Then, when it comes time to evaluate their performance, they have a yardstick at the ready.

Our favorite system of scoring is the simplest. It has four levels:

We exceeded expectations.
This means that you not only hit your target numbers, but you also far outperformed the target you set. Even accounting for ambitious goals, this amounts to a gigantic achievement. Beware, though—if you're hitting this level each time you set a goal, it probably means that you're not setting ambitious enough goals in the first place.

We delivered.
This means you hit the target that you set. OKR goals should be ambitious, so when you grade an OKR with this score, it really means that you and your team have

done exceptionally well. Though the language is modest, this score should mean that you all deserve a party— and maybe a bonus.

We fell short.
This means that you made progress, you created some value, and you can claim success. Still, you didn't achieve the ambitious goal you set out to achieve. There's room to do better. It might mean that you continue to work on this goal or that you need to consider why you fell short or both. Either way, this grade includes elements of both success and failure.

We failed to deliver.
This means that you didn't create the value that you set out to create. Sometimes, this grade reflects a sincere but failed effort to work on the OKR. Other times, this grade indicates that you and your team didn't actually focus on your goal at all. Regardless, this grade means that something went seriously wrong. And you and the team need to have some hard conversations about what happened and why.

After you've set your key results using the two conversations we describe above—what's possible and what's valuable—spend a little time creating a simple score sheet with percentage ranges aligned with each of the four grades:

- **We exceeded expectations** = Our results were **more than 100%** of our target.
- **We delivered** = Our results were **80 to 100%** of our target.

- **We fell short** = Our results were **50 to 79%** of our target.
- **We failed to deliver** = Our results were **less than 50%** of our target.

We said that we don't love the process of scoring OKRs. Why? **It's too easy for scores to become a focus of the conversation.** Sometimes, scores are even used for performance evaluation and compensation conversations. This is a mistake. **You really want the focus to stay on the results themselves, not the scores.** For this reason, many teams and organizations choose to skip scoring and focus their energy and attention on tracking the results directly.

Scoring is useful as a diagnostic tool. It's useful at the start of the OKR-setting process to help you figure out what good key results would look like. And it's useful at the end of a period to evaluate your performance and compare your performance quarter-over-quarter and year-over-year. Are you consistently underperforming? Overperforming? How might you change your goal-setting process and your work to correct that? Stick to these uses, and scoring can help you. Beyond that, keep your focus on achieving your key results.

Collaborating to Write and Align OKRs Across the Organization

So far, this chapter has focused on the process of writing your OKRs with your team. If you're in a very small organization, this might be all you need. But for most organizations, you're going to want to make sure that your OKRs work in the context of the larger organization. Writing your team's OKRs is only one part of the process, then. You also need to make sure that your OKRs align with the work and goals of your peers.

In the next chapter, we'll share with you a process to align your team OKRs with the rest of the organization.

Key Takeaways

1. To write an objective, determine the biggest problem you need to solve and what it would look like if you solved it. Keep it inspirational, qualitative, timeboxed, and specific. You should focus on one objective per quarter.

2. To write key results, use the following question as your guide: "Who does what by how much?" Your answer should reflect the kind of behavior change you want to see in your customer, as well as the rate of change needed, to achieve your objective. You should set only two or three key results per objective.

3. Your OKRs should reflect only the scope of responsibility your team has in its work.

4. Every OKR needs a parent OKR. You need to be able to connect every OKR to the higher organizational purpose.

5. When you start, it's hard to write OKRs, particularly key results. Beware of writing your key results as lists of tasks, outputs, team behaviors or actions, system behaviors, or previously agreed-upon projects. Key results should always be customer behaviors, with realistic yet ambitious target rates of change.

Chapter 7

Setting OKRs Through Collaboration

In most organizations, goal-setting is a top-down activity. Executives and managers decide on the goals, hand them down to the teams, give the teams deadlines, and say "go" without much back-and-forth. It's not surprising, then, that when organizations start working with OKRs, they fall into that familiar command and control pattern. After all, why would goal-setting with OKRs be any different?

In the 2010s, we were part of the co-founding team at Neo, a small product innovation company in New York City. After the company was acquired, the executives at the new managing company informed us that our new goal was $19 million in revenue in the next year. They needed us to hit that number for Neo to make sense in their company's portfolio, so they dropped the goal in our laps and sent us on our not-so-merry way.

We knew we couldn't hit that goal. Neo had closed the previous year with just over $3 million in revenue. We had a snowball's chance in hell of growing to $19 million just one year later. That number contradicted everything that we knew about our market, the services that we were selling, and our staff's capabilities. To use the language from the last chapter: That number wasn't possible.

The worst part of this was that, because the goal-setting process was completely top-down, we had no opportunity to share our points of view and discuss alternatives. As a result, we felt misunderstood, demoralized, and defeated, knowing that no matter what we did, we wouldn't be able to hit our goal.

Three things stand out in this scenario:

1. The logic and motivations of ownership were opaque. Our team was given only a number not an objective. What did that number mean for the parent company? What was the objective they were trying to achieve? We didn't know.
2. The people closest to the work who had the most information about the work (in this case, us) were not the ones setting goals for the work.
3. Without any input in the goal-setting process, our teams had no buy-in to the goals given to us and, therefore, much less determination to achieve them.

These are the problems with top-down goal-setting, and they are why, when organizations start using OKRs, they need to collaborate to set their goals from the top-down *and* the bottom-up.

Collaborating Top-Down *and* Bottom-Up to Set OKRs

When executives hand down goals without talking to their teams, teams often feel a sense of "Screw them for telling us what to do. We're the only ones who know what's going on." Sound familiar? Surprise: There's a better way to do it.

OKRs allow us to replace command and control leadership with alignment and autonomy. This means taking a collaborative approach to goal-setting, one in which both leadership and the teams doing the work collaborate to create OKRs that are right for them. Collaborating in this way solves the problems we outlined above and tackles strategic concerns in the following ways:

- Top-down and bottom-up collaboration leverages the knowledge and points-of-view of both leadership and teams, allowing organizations to set goals with deeper understanding.
- With more accurate, up-to-date information and a better understanding of the work, teams can help determine realistic goals that actually make sense.
- When people set their own goals, they are infinitely more motivated to hit them.
- When leadership and teams collaborate to set goals, you get goals that are both strategic and realistic, instead of one or the other.

This collaboration grants teams a sense of ownership and autonomy about their work and acknowledges their expertise and boots-on-the-ground understanding of their domains.

It's easy to be cynical—whether you're a leader or a worker—and think that *those other guys* are clueless. *People can't lead themselves!* or *Leaders have no idea!* In reality, people aren't clueless (though exchanges like the one in the Neo story can make one feel that way); they're just looking at different information and are worried about different problems. By coming together in these conversations, leadership can tell teams about the problems they're solving, teams can tell leadership about the problems *they're* solving, and the two parties can find alignment.

In the case of our Neo team, had the new owners consulted us on the goal, they could have shared their point of view. Perhaps they wanted to demonstrate growth, or maybe they believed a target like $19 million in revenue would be motivational. At the same time, we could have shared why we thought that $19 million was an unrealistic target. We could have shared our understanding of the market we were competing in, the customer needs we were serving, and our strategy. We were a young business looking for product-market fit. We weren't ready to scale.

This conversation would probably have revealed a deeply misaligned set of strategic assumptions. Ownership wanted a high-growth business, whereas we were looking for product-market fit. That's what we should have been talking about—not revenue targets! Ultimately, we could have saved everyone a lot of time and headaches by having a collaborative conversation to reach a consensus on what was best for everyone in the process.

A Process for Top-Down and Bottom-Up Collaboration

Let's look quickly at a process that you can use with leadership to set your goals. It starts with finding clarity about the strategy that you're pursuing.

The ideal process for setting OKRs collaboratively goes something like this:

1. **Top-down:** Leadership determines the strategy and high-level OKRs for the organization and communicates them clearly to every team and every individual.

2. **Bottom-up:** Each team creates its own OKRs that fall within its sphere of influence, have a clear relationship to a parent OKR, and function to advance for the organization's high-level OKRs.

3. **Collaboration:** All teams bring their OKRs to their leaders and peer teams and explain why they chose their goals and how they believe achieving those goals will help the organization reach its high-level OKRs.

4. **Revise and publish:** Following the collaborative conversations, teams revise their OKRs as needed, then publish their final OKRs for the period.

Creating Alignment

In the previous chapters, we described the first two steps of this process. Now, once you have your teams' first draft OKRs, it's time for the third step: collaboration, in which you share your OKRs with your leaders and your peer teams. Every organization's process is a little different, but we want to suggest some questions you should be asking, in conversations both with leaders and with your peer teams.

Talking to Leadership

When reviewing your OKRs with your leaders, you want to get their blessing about your focus and your strategy. To do that, make sure to hit these points in your conversation:

- Be prepared to tell the story of why you believe that your OKR is the right area of focus for your team. Tell them your strategy, starting with your obstacle, and how you intend to approach that obstacle.
- Tell them why, of all of the things that you *could* be working on, this is the right thing.
- Tell them how this supports the organization's OKRs. Make sure that you can connect your OKR to a parent OKR (as we described above).
- Confirm that your leaders agree with your key results. Are they ambitious enough? Too bold?
- Ask them to consider whether or not there are other teams you'll need to work with to accomplish your goals. Are there peer teams for whom they are responsible and with whom you'll need to coordinate? Are there other teams who depend on you for things— and if so, might those things interfere with your plans?

Talking to Your Peer Teams

As you began the process of writing your OKRs, you considered your scope of control. During the discussion with your leaders, you (hopefully) identified any peer teams or teams with whom you had dependencies. If you didn't create a shared OKR with these teams, this is the moment to check in with them. Here are some topics for discussion:

- What do you need from them, or them from you? Will these dependencies prevent either team from being successful with their OKRs?
- Are you working on complementary things? Are your approaches compatible? Do either or both teams need to adjust their approach?
- Are you working on two different parts of the same problem? Would it make sense for you to share a single OKR?

The Difficulty of Making the Case for Your Goals

Though goal-setting works best for teams when it's a collaborative effort, it's not necessarily as straightforward as it sounds. In those conversations with leaders, teams need to be able to make the connection between the customer behaviors they're working on and the end goals of the company. **They need to tell a compelling story about their proposed OKRs that will ultimately prompt the leadership team to approve their goals.**

Revise and Publish

Once you've had these conversations, you can expect to do some revision and adjustment. The key here is to make sure that your processes don't take too long. Don't spend months trying to get everyone's OKRs perfect. Make quick decisions and then get to work. Remember, in addition to creating focus, autonomy, and alignment, we're also trying to be agile. So move quickly and expect to change course as you learn more.

When you've revised your work, share it widely within your organization. Post it on your cubicle wall. Share it on your team's Wiki page. Add it to whatever shared communication tools you use in your company. We'll talk about this in more depth in Parts 3 and 4 of this book, but for now, remember that we benefit from creating transparency around our OKRs.

Key Takeaways

1. OKRs require both top-down and bottom-up collaboration between leadership and individual teams across the organization. This collaboration grants teams a sense of ownership over their work and acknowledges their expertise while allowing leaders to ensure that the teams' work remains aligned with the organization's strategy and focused on the right things.
2. Teams must be able to connect their work with the larger organizational goals. This means both being able to tell a compelling and logical story *and* having access to the data to back that story up.

Chapter 8

Common Questions About Writing OKRs

Just about everyone who writes OKRs wrestles with a common set of questions and issues. This is true whether you're doing it for the first time or whether you've got a lot of experience. These questions generally fall into three categories:

General Questions About OKRs
- How many OKRs should we have?
- Should everything get an OKR?
- At what level should we write our OKRs?
- Where do the numbers come from?
- We can't measure the key result we want to write. Should we write it anyway?
- Does every key result have to be an outcome? Every time? Really?

Questions About Teams
- Should we have individual OKRs?
- Does every team need its own OKRs?
- Should OKRs be cross-functional, or should each discipline have its own?

Questions About Customers

- I make internally facing products.
  Why do I need OKRs?
- I don't work directly with customers. What should I do?
- Our company is B2B. How do OKRs work for us?

We'll answer all of these questions over the course of this chapter.

General Questions About OKRs

How many OKRs should we have?

You should focus on one main objective for each quarter. For each objective, we recommend setting two or three key results.

One of the most important reasons to use OKRs in the first place is to create focus. You can't focus on more than one thing. This is particularly true with your objective. Narrow things down by determining the most important problem you have to solve right now. You may have many problems, but you have only one *most important* problem. This is where you focus at this moment. It doesn't mean you ignore the other issues. It does mean you're not focused on them for now.

We have rarely seen any team successfully focus on and achieve more than one OKR. Teams that have multiple OKRs are often spread too thin to achieve any of them. They constantly struggle to prioritize work because choosing to focus on one means neglecting the other.

At the organizational level, you want to have a small set of OKRs—probably two or three—that represent different dimensions of your business. Or, if you're a big organization, you might want to have one OKR per business unit or other major division. Regardless, we think that when you're starting your OKR journey, less is more. Start with one and build from there.

Should everything get an OKR?

Make a distinction between important *business as usual* work and OKRs.

If OKRs focus you on one important thing, then what should you do with the other day-to-day things that you're responsible for? After all, you need to keep the business up and running, right?

Most organizations distinguish between OKRs and Business as Usual (BAU) metrics. BAU metrics cover operational activities, like the reliability and stability of the company website, the operations of the company's campus, or the performance of the call center. The idea of BAU is broad enough to cover any important day-to-day responsibility that falls outside of your focus area.

In her book *Radical Focus*, OKR expert Christina Wodtke calls these kinds of metrics "heartbeat metrics." She recommends that you should be paying attention to these metrics in an ongoing way, and that they should be a part of every check-in meeting, but that they remain separate from the metrics you've selected for your key results.

At what level should we write our OKRs?

Write OKR statements within your scope of control.

As teams start writing their objectives and key results, they often ask at what level they should be writing their OKRs. Level-setting speaks to the scope of your team's work—the part of the product or customer's journey that you work on. Do you work on something with a broad scope or a narrow one? For instance, do you oversee multiple client advertising accounts or just the analytics for one large account? Are you in charge of the whole mortgage application process or just document verification? This, as you may recall from earlier chapters, is your scope of control.

Often, teams see the organizational OKRs and keep thinking big-picture as they write their own, setting OKRs for things like revenue, perhaps because they're worried that the goal they choose may not be "big enough" for their stakeholders. The thing is, you can't sign up for goals you can't directly influence—and it won't do you or the company any good if you try to. Instead, **only write OKR statements within your sphere of influence.**

If you work at a leadership level and are in charge of a whole product, program, business unit, or even the company, your team's OKRs should reflect that entire entity. Since you have responsibility for the whole thing (the teams within the business unit and their dependencies as well as your priorities and resources), a product- or program-level goal is appropriate for you. In these positions, your OKRs will often be the high-level OKRs with high-level measures, such as revenue, sales, or customer satisfaction serving as key results.

If, however, you work on a team with a more focused area of responsibility, you likely can influence only one slice of the customer journey. You need to set goals for the specific piece of the puzzle for which you and your team are responsible—and only that piece. As an example, if you work in a hospital doing intake of new patients, your OKR is going to focus on efficient and accurate patient onboarding. Your OKR should not reflect the quality of care a patient receives or whether they have to visit the hospital again in the near future. Those key results are outside of your control. The same holds true for revenue goals. If the work you do directly influences your company's revenue, by all means sign up for a key result with a revenue number attached to it. But if your main focus is ensuring that customers can seamlessly authenticate into your system, your work does not directly influence revenue. Your OKRs should reflect authentication success rates only.

Where do the numbers come from?
Choose numbers that are realistic but also ambitious enough to make a difference to the organization.

Sometimes, attaching numbers to your key results is relatively straightforward. Perhaps you've been given a target to hit, and you have a model that you can use to work out the numbers to get to that target. You might have a revenue target, for example, and you can use that to set a sales target for your key result. If you find yourself in this position, consider yourself lucky.

More often, you won't really have a clear model to guide you. Sometimes, that's because you're doing something new, so there's no historical data to work with. Or it might be that you have data, but you're not sure how much of a change you should target. In our experience, this is the situation that most teams find themselves in—even though they'd like to pretend otherwise.

So, here's the dirty little secret of goal-setting: It's OK to guess. Really. Now, when we say "guess" here, we mean that it's OK to make an *informed* guess, based on everything that you currently know about the problem that you're working on. Take a guess, then talk to your colleagues, peers, and stakeholders. Have honest conversations. Ask, *If we hit this number, will this be valuable?* And, *Is this ambitious enough?* And, *Is this plausible?* Remember, you're going for numbers that both are realistic and will make a difference to your organization.

Once you begin working with your OKR, you'll start to learn more about the problem, and you'll have a chance to refine your numbers.

(For more on this topic, see Chapter 6.)

We can't measure the key result we want to write. Should we write it anyway?

If you think it's important, write that key result. You'll figure out how to measure it.

Sometimes the customer behavior that seems most important is difficult to measure. Maybe people aren't doing it yet. Perhaps it takes place in a physical space that you can't access, so getting accurate measures will be difficult, or even impossible. Regardless of the challenges in measuring the outcome that matters to you, write it as your key result anyway. If this metric is important to the business—and you can tell a compelling story around it—the organization will help you figure out a way to measure it or determine what you can use as an indicator in the meantime. Perhaps instead of quantitative data, you can start with qualitative data derived from surveys or interviews. Or maybe there's a leading indicator for the behavior that you can measure. Start there while you figure out how you can get to the desired metric.

Does every key result have to be an outcome? Every time? Really?

Yes, every one, every time.

You want your key results to be expressed as outcomes. *Who does what by how much?*

It's tempting to express your key result as an output—a thing that you're committing to make. The problem here is that you can make your output—and even make it on time, on budget, and meeting all the requirements—and still not create any value. (Remember Google Glass?) The moment your key result becomes an output, your team stops working on the problem of creating value. Instead, your team is working on a fixed-scope, fixed-time initiative to deliver a thing that might or might not work.

Let's be clear: *Key results should never be outputs.*

We use OKRs to focus on creating value. Key results as outputs neuter the true value of OKRs.

Now, we're sometimes tempted to consider using high-level "impact" metrics as key results, especially when writing organizational OKRs. After all, "grow revenue by 30%" seems like a valid goal. But we've never seen a situation where this same goal can't be expressed as a customer-centric outcome. "Customer purchases grow by 30%" is the same goal, expressed as an outcome, and has the benefit of re-emphasizing customers.

So yeah, every one. Every time.

Questions About Teams

Should we have individual OKRs?

No. Keep OKRs at the team level.

We cover this topic in detail in Chapter 14, so we'll keep it brief here. You should not have individual OKRs. OKRs are at their most effective when they're set for a team or for larger groups.

Does every team need its own OKRs?

No, in some cases, teams can share OKRs.

Dependent teams can share an OKR and work together to achieve it. This is a good scaling strategy that reduces the number of OKRs an organization needs to manage. If some of those dependent teams don't use OKRs, it's important to set expectations up front about how your style of work may differ and decide on a communication cadence and format. (This question is covered in detail in both Chapters 5 and 6.)

Should OKRs be cross-functional, or should each discipline have its own?

OKRs should not be discipline-centric. They should be cross-functional.

The default approach for all OKRs is that they should be set for an entire cross-functional team responsible for the delivery of some product or service into the market. That works when you're organized this way, but sometimes, organizations aren't set up well for cross-functional collaboration.

You've also got teams that are "horizontal" or "services" teams, organized around specific disciplines and designed to work with other teams to provide a specific function or skill. These could be designers, lawyers, marketers, or compliance specialists, to name a few. So though cross-functional, market-facing teams can create straightforward OKRs related to what they're building, discipline-oriented teams struggle to adopt OKRs.

The Problems Faced by "Support" Teams

We spoke recently with a group of people on a communications and marketing team at an organization we consult with. They shared their struggles coming up with goals that made sense for them.

"We're not really on any of the project teams," they told us. "We support them when they need us, and then we move on to another project. How do we account for our contribution to the project in an OKR?"

We heard the same thing from a design leader: "How do we set OKRs for the design portion of the work?" In both cases, OKRs felt irrelevant to the discipline-specific team because they, and the organization, saw their work as a service being provided to the overall initiative rather than an integral part of the success of that initiative.

Discipline-Specific OKRs

Here are four ways in which discipline-specific OKRs can make sense.

Option 1: Make the product better.
When we think about these horizontal disciplines as service providers, there are three ways their work can be accounted for with objectives and key results. The first option is to include them as part of the whole team's goals. In other words, the initiative team's OKRs are the service team's OKRs as well. The designers, communication folks, or platform engineers function as a full-time part of the team. Their goals are the team's goals. They win or lose together. There is no division between the "initiative" goals and the "service team" goals. They work together, as a cohesive unit, to make the product better.

When we carve out discipline-specific goals, we divide the team. We break the shared purpose and alignment. As a result, you get teams that are optimizing locally for the work they're doing. A designer could say, "I did my five revisions and three customer interviews, and the customers we spoke with gave the work a strong thumbs-up." At this point, the designer has washed their hands clean of the product; the way it's implemented, deployed, marketed, and ultimately used by customers is not important to them. They "did their work." The feasibility of their work is not something they're concerned about because their goal is to deliver good design work. This is how they're measured.

Option 2: Make the discipline team better.
The second option for discipline-specific OKRs is to set internally facing goals designed to improve the team itself. For example, you could set an objective to make the communications team the "most desirable communications team in your industry." You could set key results that measure things like retention of current employees and referrals of new

employees from existing team members. Goals set this way focus on creating a great practice, regardless of which product the team works on.

In this case, the goals make a better organization. Ultimately, that organization should help make better products. In this case, however, we're only measuring the health of the discipline.

Option 3: Make the discipline's (internal) customers better.

The third option for setting OKRs for a specific discipline team is to focus on that team's customers. Who consumes the things created by the communications team, for example? What about the design team's output— who uses that to do their job? If we examine this from the perspective that everyone has a customer, we measure the changes in the behavior of our internal colleagues who work with us.

For example, designers on software teams need to communicate their ideas to software developers. We could write an OKR that looks like this:

> **Objective:**
> *Make it as easy as possible for developers to start writing code before the holiday season starts.*
>
> **Key Result:**
> *Developers spend 75% less time clarifying design direction.*

Thinking about our colleagues as customers helps us continuously improve the way we do our specific jobs. Maybe prototypes aren't more effective than sketching together on a whiteboard and having a conversation. Using OKRs in this way helps us figure these things out and makes us examine how we can keep getting better.

Option 4: All three options at the same time

The three options are not mutually exclusive. You can set internally facing goals while also having your team members work with their cross-functional colleagues to make better products. You can also continuously improve your own work at the same time. In fact, this is the way you should work. This way, you're not only making the product better, but you're also continuously assessing how well you're leading your specific discipline and how you can improve it and the work the teams in your discipline do.

Questions About Customers

I make internally facing products. Why do I need OKRs?

You need OKRs because you still have customers—the internal people who use your products—and you can focus your work on helping them do their jobs better.

Internally facing products, like scheduling systems, reporting and analytics programs, or identity management systems, have customers, too. The customers are the employees of your company who use them. In these cases, the customers you service need to perform their job better. Your key results reflect positive changes in the way these colleagues do their jobs. OKRs make perfect sense in this case as they give internal product teams clear measures of success for these products. This is another clear example of one of our key mantras: Everyone has a customer.

I don't work directly with customers. What should I do?

If you really don't work with end customers, your OKRs should probably focus on internal customers, as we've recommended throughout this book. Sometimes though, it makes sense for your OKR to focus on an end customer, even though you work at some distance from them. In that case, what should you do?

Ask colleagues with customer access to help you or start your own customer research effort.

This question comes up a lot in large organizations with complex structures. Many employees don't have direct access to end customers, making measuring behavior change difficult. One way to handle this is to reach out to your colleagues who do have access to the customer. Explain to them what you're trying to learn and measure, and ask how they can help you get the data you need.

Another option is to reach out to your company's market research or data analysis teams. Share the work you're doing and what you need to know to do your job well, and see if there is a cadence within which they could provide you with some data and insight.

One last option: Start your own customer outreach effort. Just because you don't work directly with customers doesn't mean you shouldn't be able to speak with them. An organization that has chosen to implement OKRs is working toward becoming more customer-centric. Your request to have access to customers is a good step in that direction.

Our organization is B2B. How do OKRs work for us?

You're still targeting customers, but only *your* customers—the businesses who buy *your* products and services—not *their* customers.

OKRs work in business-to-business (B2B) environments in exactly the same way they do in consumer-facing organizations, with one exception: The humans whose behavior you are trying to change are the people in your client organizations who buy and use the products you provide.

In B2B environments, it's typical to be in a situation where your customers have customers of their own. It might be tempting to think that your job is to help your customers succeed with their customers. In a way, it is—but you need to be careful here. You can't be responsible for your customer's customers. So the mistake you want to avoid is setting key results that measure the behavior of your customer's customers.

Once you deliver your product to your customers, it's up to them to do the right thing with *their* customers. They need to use your product or service to do the right thing with *their* customers—to market it correctly, price it correctly, deliver it correctly, use it correctly, etc. All of these factors affect how *their* customers behave. But you can't be responsible for those behaviors because you don't influence them. Instead, you need to focus on the buyers, implementers, and internal users of *your* products and whether or not you're making them more successful.

Common Pitfalls to Avoid When Writing OKRs

It's easy to make mistakes when you start any new process or way of working. We get it! There are many new pieces to wrap your head around. But with OKRs, some of the most common mistakes happen when writing key results—largely because writing key results involves shifting your mindset from focusing on output to focusing on outcomes. It takes some getting used to.

Here are the most common (and most detrimental) pitfalls to avoid when writing your OKRs:

Writing Key Results as Task Lists

One of the most common pitfalls we see when people start writing OKRs is that they completely miss the whole outcomes-as–key results piece and make their key results a list of tasks. Sometimes this happens because leaders like predictability. They want a straight answer when they ask, "What are you going to build or work on next?" Teams inevitably write their key results to be able to satisfy this question. But task lists focus on output and task completion, which, as you know by now, is the opposite of what OKRs focus on.

Another common mistake managers and teams make is thinking that actions, like "launch the marketing campaign" or "design 10 subway ads," are human behaviors and therefore must be key results. Technically, "launching" a campaign and "designing" ads *are* human behaviors—but they're *your* behaviors, not your customers'. When they're your behaviors, they reflect tactics—or outputs—that your team could deploy in the hopes of impacting customer behavior. By contrast, you need to focus on the *ways* those tactics could influence customer behavior. For example, "What do you hope people will *do* when they see the subway ads?" That's your key result. No solidified outputs, tactics, products, programs, or initiatives of any sort should appear in your key results. Period.

Reverse Engineering Key Results to Fit Your To-do List

You'd be hard-pressed to find any organization, especially a high-growth company, that doesn't have a to-do list or backlog of work that's predefined, prioritized, and in some stage of development before it starts using OKRs. This makes for an interesting challenge when the new goal-setting framework refocuses everyone's work on outcomes instead of outputs.

Why? People wonder (and worry about) what will happen to the work they're already doing. Oftentimes, a lot of work has gone into building consensus and alignment around the tasks or projects they planned, and people don't want to "throw away" their efforts. They may also have made commitments to deliver these previously planned tasks.

Employees also tend to distrust that leadership will evaluate them on outcomes achieved instead of work completed or products delivered. Sometimes these fears come into play because leaders haven't changed the incentive structure or performance evaluation criteria—or they haven't fully communicated or supported the cultural shifts required for OKRs to work well. (For more on that, head to Chapter 15.) So, to circumvent any potential issues, teams sometimes shape their OKRs in a way that captures items on their old to-do list, even if these items don't align with their new objective.

The thing is, writing OKRs to fit your preexisting to-do list renders them ineffective. Your list of "OKRs" grows longer and longer, which makes it more and more difficult to achieve any of the goals you've set for yourself. And because it's often easier for stakeholders to measure "progress" by output, teams tend to slip back into old habits, working solely according to their old task lists, and OKRs get ignored.

Writing Key Results as Measures of System Behavior

As we've said, key results should be metrics—i.e., numbers, percentages, or ratios. But that doesn't mean any numbers will do. One pitfall teams often fall into is using any metric they can come up with as long as it has a percentage, thinking, "It has a % sign, so it must be a good key result." However, they fail to look further at *who* is performing the behavior represented in the number they've selected.

For instance, one team at a supermarket company we worked with once wrote the following key result: "50% of the products on our shelves will be store-brand products." In another session, the web development team of a government agency wrote, "Reduce homepage load time by 80%." In both cases, the teams were confident they'd done well. After all, they specified numbers—more precisely, percentages—and those percentages were related to the usage of their "systems." Importantly, though, the usage wasn't measuring what their *customers* did; rather, it measured what their systems or products did or how they functioned. The percentage of store-brand products is a feature of the store, not the shopper. Homepage load time is a feature of the website, not the user. Both of these features may drive customer behavior, but they are not measures of what people do. Though the metric of system behavior may help you determine what project you want to do next, it will not help you determine if you've delivered any value.

When you write your key results, it's important to **scrutinize the metrics you set to ensure they measure *customer* behavior, not system behavior or product performance**.

Let's look at the supermarket example: "50% of products on our shelves will be store-brand products." Where is the customer (the "who") in this sentence? Not there. You have to go deeper: What is it that you want to achieve by making 50% of the products store-brand? Let's say it's an increase in same-store visits from recurring customers and average order value. Where is the customer in that sentence? Everywhere. The customer is the one making repeat visits to the store and buying more products per visit. Those are the customer behaviors you want to target in your key results. You *might* be able to get there by increasing store-brand products, but you might not. There are many variables to work with. But if that's your goal, that's what you target—not the metric of system behavior that you assume will deliver the result you want.

Remember, every key result your team generates should fit into this template:

[Who] [does what] [by how much]?

The [who] *must* be a customer. Let's try it:

[Store-brand products] [grow in representative
proportion on our shelves] [to equal 50%].
This is NOT a customer action.

[Our customers] [choose store-brand products]
[50% of the time] when presented with an alternative.
This IS a customer action!

Another way to think about the question is to frame it as, "What will people be doing differently if we do a great job?" Whatever behavior we're
looking for is what we're targeting by improving system functionality.
That's our measure of success. That's a good key result.

Sandbagging Key Results

"Sandbagging" is a term used to describe the act (and sometimes art) of
under-promising and over-delivering. It means setting goals you know
you can hit easily so that when the end of the quarter hits, you crush
your targets. Praise, promotions, and accolades ensue—even though you
didn't really accomplish as much as it seems like you did.

Praise aside, why do some teams sandbag their key results? Similar
to when teams reverse engineer their key results, sandbagging allows
them to continue working more or less as usual and avoid the discomfort
of changing their processes. If it ain't broke, don't fix it, right?

The problem is, with technological advances, processes naturally
become less efficient and effective over time. Teams that sandbag their
key results typically don't challenge themselves to stretch their capabilities, look for new efficiencies in their work, or find new techniques to
gain more customer feedback. As a result, their agility diminishes. When
the time comes for them to respond adeptly to a sharp, unexpected shift
in the market—and that time always comes—they're unable to do so.

Alternatively, teams may set the bar for their key results low
because their leaders haven't changed the way they evaluate employee
performance. If compensations, bonuses, and promotions are tied to
OKR achievement, *not* hitting OKRs could threaten their employment or

exclude them from promotions. When that's the case, sandbagging is a no-brainer.

To avoid it, leaders need to decouple OKR achievement and compensation, reset expectations around key results and achievement, and establish psychological safety so employees can bring forward questions, concerns, and failures without fear of retaliation. (Leader readers, see Chapter 14.) The targets you set for your key results should have around a 20 to 25% cushion—meaning, you should expect to reach 75 to 80% of your goal metrics. The rest is a "nice to have," though teams should see that cushion as an opportunity to stretch their thinking and try to come up with new, creative ways to hit their targets.

Key Takeaways

1. Answers to general OKR questions, in rapid-fire:
   a. Teams should have one main objective for each quarter and two or three key results per objective.
   b. Teams should only write OKRs that focus on work within their scope of control.
   c. For key results, you should choose numbers that are realistic, but also ambitious enough to make a difference to the organization.
   d. Even if you can't easily measure the outcome you've chosen to target in your key results, if it's the most important and valuable outcome for you to pursue to achieve your objective, choose it anyway. You'll figure out how to measure it as you go.
   e. Every key result needs to be an outcome. Every time.

2. Answers to questions about teams
   using OKRs, in rapid-fire:
   a. OKRs should only be written at the team level
      or for larger groups, not for individuals.
   b. Not every team needs its own set of OKRs.
      Sometimes it makes sense for teams to share
      OKRs. They should, however, be cross-functional,
      not discipline-specific (with a few exceptions).

3. Answers to questions about the role of
   customers with OKRs, in rapid-fire:
   a. Internally facing teams need OKRs because
      they still have customers—the internal
      people who use their products—and they
      can use OKRs to focus their work on helping
      these people do their jobs better.
   b. If you don't work directly with customers or have
      direct access to customer data to inform your
      key results targets, ask for help from teams that
      do—or start your own customer research efforts.
   c. In B2B environments, your customers
      are the businesses buying your products
      and/or services, not *their* customers. Your
      work focuses on the businesses.

4. The most common pitfalls teams encounter when
   writing OKRs are as follows: writing key results
   as task lists, reverse engineering key results to fit
   your team's to-do lists, choosing key results that are
   measures of system behavior instead of customer
   behavior, and sandbagging key results metrics.

Part 3

Using OKRs

In the first chapter of the book, we said that OKRs are three things: a goal-setting framework, a process, and a culture. We talked about the goal-setting framework in the last part of the book. Now, we're going to talk about **OKRs as a process**. We'll call that process the **OKR Cycle**.

In this section of the book, we'll teach you about this cycle, a simple and powerful way to organize your work. We'll describe the cycle and show you how to use it.

When you're really using the OKR Cycle, though, OKRs change the way that you approach your work, encouraging a more experimental and customer-centric way of working. We'll dig into that as well.

For us, these ideas are some of the most powerful and exciting parts of OKRs, and we're excited to share them with you.

Chapter 9

The OKR Cycle

What does it mean to *use* OKRs? At the most basic level, it means that we use them on a daily, weekly, monthly, quarterly, and annual basis to **decide what to work on**. In many cases, it also means that we **change** *how* **we work**, leaning more into short cycles of testing and learning and measuring our results as we move forward.

To do this, most companies that work with OKRs have implemented some version of the **OKR Cycle**. This cycle defines the activities associated with using OKRs, from strategy setting to OKR writing to the regular rhythm of meetings used to review progress.

In this chapter, we're looking at the overall process of the OKR Cycle at a high level. We'll describe the big milestones and events in the cycle.

The OKR Cycle

The OKR Cycle is simply the rhythm that we use to work with OKRs within our organizations. Although it varies somewhat from organization to organization—and you can adapt it to make it work for your specific needs—it has the following pieces.

1. Organizational Strategy and OKRs
2. Team OKRs
3. Execution
4. Learning
5. Checking In

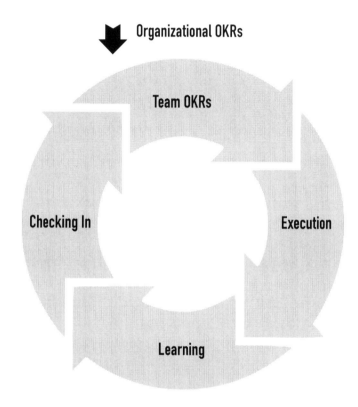

Let's take a brief look at each one of these pieces.

1: Organizational Strategy and OKRs

The process begins with setting organizational strategy and goals, as we've described in Part 2 of this book. This happens annually each year.

2: Setting Team-Level OKRs

The process continues, again as we've described earlier. Teams will set their OKRs annually and revisit them during their quarterly check-ins (see below).

3: Execution

Once our goals are set, we get to work, pursuing the goals as defined by our OKRs. As we've said, OKRs don't tell teams what to do—they only define success. So teams are free to figure out how to achieve that success. That means that this phase of work is based on the idea that teams will need to figure out what to work on in order to achieve their results.

You might have a good hunch about what's going to create that success. With your team, you can choose to pursue it. Or perhaps your team has been asked to complete a set of tasks that you didn't define—perhaps your team has been given direction from leadership about what to do, perhaps a set of things that you're obliged to deliver.

One of the most magical properties of OKRs is that the only thing that matters is results. So if you're working through a list of tasks that are not creating results, OKRs give you permission, based on the evidence, to shake up that task list. If you're pursuing your hunch, OKRs allow you to do that, as long as you're creating key results.

To create discipline, this phase, **execution**, is timeboxed. You work on something until your next check-in meeting, at which point you evaluate the results you've generated. If this work has been fruitful, great. But if not, you'll use the conversations at the check-in to decide what to do about it. (And because check-in meetings happen frequently, you limit the time spent working on things that are not working, thus limiting your risk.)

In practice, then, this phase of work is different from business as usual. Instead of working on projects for long periods of time in the hopes that they'll bear fruit in the future, you restructure the work so that it looks more like a series of small tests, all designed to generate results, or if that's not possible, to generate evidence that you're on the right path.

There are many names for this way of working. Probably the most popular (and most misunderstood) is *Agile*. It turns out that OKRs are one of the best frameworks for encouraging real agility.[11] We'll talk more about this in Chapter 10.

4: Learning

Sometimes, you know exactly what you need to do to create results. That's great. You should get started and monitor your results. Sometimes, though, you're not sure about the best way to generate results. You might have a list of promising ideas, but if you're honest with yourself and your teammates, you'll admit that you're not sure the ideas will work. Other times, you get started on something, and as you monitor your progress, it becomes clear that the idea isn't working as well as you had hoped. This is where *learning activities* come in.

Sometimes called research or discovery, this refers to the learning tactics that you can use to test your ideas and learn why they're working or not working. This is also the part of the work through which we get to know our customers better. What are they trying to do? What's getting in their way? How might we help them be more successful?

To be honest, we debated whether or not to describe learning as a separate piece of the cycle, or whether it was just a part of the execution piece. We see learning and execution as tightly connected—in a way that

---

11 One of the most widely used and abused terms in the corporate and technology world today is "Agile." Originally proposed as a way for small tech teams to make more valuable products by using evidence and learning, it is too often today understood as a set of steps to be followed with unquestioning obedience. We're big believers in the promise of *real* agile, and we see OKRs as a tool for enabling agility inside organizations.

you can't really separate them. In other words, in the same way that you want to always be executing the work, you should also always be learning. Probably the best way to think about this is that both types of work are continuous, and you move between them in an iterative loop—a loop that happens at the heart of the OKR Cycle.

We'll go into more detail about executing and learning in Chapter 10.

5: Checking In

Your team holds regular check-in meetings to review your progress. These meetings function as punctuation in the continuous flow of the OKR Cycle. They are the ritual that you and your team use to mark the end of the timeboxed periods of executing and learning.

Most organizations use two different kinds of check-ins: monthly and quarterly. The monthly check-ins are smaller and less formal. You gather your team, immediate stakeholders, and key collaborators to look at the results you've generated so far, share what you've learned along the way, evaluate your progress, and then decide on any adjustments you might need to make to your tactics. This is an important ritual because it creates transparency and accountability.

Quarterly check-ins tend to be more structured, with a greater emphasis on strategic course correction. The logic here is that you set your OKRs three months ago—perhaps things have changed since then. Perhaps you've learned something that would cause you to reevaluate not just your tactics, but your OKR itself. Most organizations use quarterly check-ins as the opportunity to either recommit to their OKRs, adjust them if necessary, or in some cases, even discard them and write new ones.

We'll go into more detail about check-ins in Chapter 10.

Communication Is Key

The crucial element underlying every stage of the OKR Cycle is communication—consistent, continuous, transparent communication among all stakeholders. That, of course, means fellow team members, managers, and leaders, but it also means adjacent or dependent teams working toward the same goals. Monthly and quarterly check-ins are formal opportunities for these discussions, but they are by no means the only time that communication happens during the cycle. For OKRs to be effective, teams should be communicating about their work, findings, and progress at all times—daily, weekly, monthly, etc.

Consistent communication ensures four important things:

1. Communication facilitates **transparency**, which allows team members to make faster, more informed decisions as their work progresses.
2. A team's work stays in **alignment** with that of other teams and the organizational goals.
3. Leadership stays aware of what teams are working on and learning, which helps them trust teams and continue supporting their **autonomous work**.
4. Teams across the organization can share and benefit from the insights of their colleagues, allowing for even greater **alignment**, **customer-centricity**, and **agility** at all levels.

Why Work in a Cycle at All?

We live in a world of continuous change. The rate at which we receive and learn new information today is unprecedented. This means that old-fashioned work plans that unfold predictably over a year or two or five are risky endeavors. Those plans, however well-thought-out, rarely proceed unchanged. Instead, we face new developments, new learning, new market conditions, and new technological disruptions on a regular and repeated basis. We need a way to govern our work that responds to these changes and allows us to adjust quickly. This is why thinking and planning in cycles is so helpful.

The OKR Cycle is built around short intervals of work, punctuated by check-ins. This helps ensure that the team's focus is where it needs to be, on the goals they set. It also ensures that the entire organization's interdependent goals are still aligned, despite the many moving parts.

Finally, since the OKR Cycle includes continuous evaluation, it helps the whole organization stay agile, in the truest sense of the word.

Continuous Learning

The OKR Cycle rotates around one shared question: Is our work making a difference for the people we serve?

Answering that question requires that we build continuous learning activities into our work. This allows us to learn from our customers and make changes to our work *right away*. Cycles—particularly shorter ones—serve us well in this case. The shorter the cycle, the faster we learn if we're on the right path. The faster we learn, the less we invest in an idea before committing to further work in this direction. Lower investment makes course correction easier. It simply "hurts" less to change course after days or weeks of effort than after a year.

Instead of trying to predict the future and organizing our work plans for months and years at a time, working in cycles allows us to test ideas, gain insight, and then iterate to make it better. When we make course corrections based on evidence, we're **being agile**. In a continuously changing world, agility is the greatest skill we can have.

Key Takeaways

1. The OKR Cycle includes five stages, including defining the organizational strategy and OKRs, setting team-level OKRs, execution, learning, and checking in.

2. Since most organizations operate on annual cycles, it's typical to set one strategy and a set of organizational OKRs that last the full year. Teams inside the organization typically operate OKR Cycles on a quarterly basis, making it possible to assess progress and make changes to their OKRs based on what they learn at multiple points during the year.

3. For the OKR Cycle to work to its full potential, teams must communicate constantly—among themselves, with other teams and business units, and with their leaders. Communication facilitates transparency, which facilitates alignment and informed decision-making—all of which drives increased agility and customer-centricity.

Chapter 10

Working with OKRs

You may have noticed that an important piece of the puzzle is missing from your OKRs: They don't contain solutions to your problems. They aren't task lists. They aren't project plans. They aren't specifications or requirements. They aren't to-do lists. They don't tell you what to do or to make. Which means that you have to figure all that out. That may sound like a problem, but it's actually the exact thing that makes OKRs so powerful.

Why? Well, it flips the standard way we assign work on its head. Typically, leaders tell workers what to do, and workers just have to get it done. But with OKRs, the organization is essentially aligning everyone around *solving problems*. This change means that the people who are closest to the work are given permission—they're required, actually—to find the best way to do the work and solve the problem. In other words, because OKRs don't contain solutions, working with them means you have to figure out the best way to achieve the objective and generate the key results.

The Heartbeat of the OKR Cycle: Learning and Execution

So, if OKRs don't tell you what to do, then how do you figure out what to do? You do that by starting with the key result and then working backward. Remember, our key result is an outcome—a change in human behavior. So you ask: How might we create that behavior change? You make a list of options, and then you begin working through those options—executing, testing, learning, measuring, and adjusting. If your work is generating positive results, then you keep going. If it's not, you try to learn why, and sometimes, you pivot. This iterative process is the heartbeat of the OKR Cycle. It's the pulse.

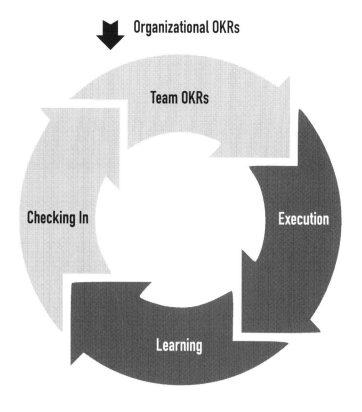

Reducing Uncertainty and Increasing Speed

OKRs give us the opportunity to improve the quality of our work, increase our speed to market and to value, and let us reduce risks along the way. We can do all of this by adopting an experimental mindset in our work.

Creating Value Sooner

In traditional project management, the work is done when we finish making the thing we said we'd make. We've built a house or a road or a new piece of software. Working with OKRs and outcomes is different. Our goal is customer-centric, to change people's behaviors by introducing positive value. So "When are we done?" is not the right question. The better question is: **How soon can we start creating value?**

Remember the donut store from Chapter 5? Let's say that one of our key results is to increase foot traffic to the store. How, exactly, are we going to do that?

This is actually the first question we face when we're using OKRs. After we set our goals, we may not be sure how to change our customers' behavior. We often *believe* we know how to do that; we usually have ideas that we think will get us there. Sometimes, we guess right, but sometimes we guess wrong. Often, it's just hard to know what will work best (and to admit that).

Imagine that you're the donut store owner. You might hire an advertising firm to create some ads to run in the local newspaper. The ads will take about a month to develop. You probably won't see any change in foot traffic until the ads have been running for a week or so. This means that it will be five or six weeks until you see foot traffic increase, if you see any increase at all.

On the other hand, you could hire a person—maybe your neighbor's teenage son or daughter—to stand on the corner with a sign that directs people to your store. They could start tomorrow. You'd be able to see value immediately—if it works, that is.

Which idea is better: an ad agency or a teenager with a sign? Here's the problem: We don't know.

An **Experimental** *Mindset*

This is a general truth about working with outcomes. It's usually diffi-cult to be truly certain of the way forward. This is an uncomfortable idea, kind of an emperor's new clothes situation. In most workplaces, it's hard (and not always safe) to admit to doubt and uncertainty. Just because we don't like to admit it, though, doesn't change the situation. Humans are strange and complex and unpredictable, and the business of changing people's behavior is, too. There's just a lot of uncertainty.

The best way to approach this problem is to adopt an experimental mindset. This means that we want to bring a test-and-learn approach to our work. If we hire the neighbor's teenager, we might only do it on a trial basis for a week to see if it generates a lift in foot traffic. At the same time, we might hire an ad agency to do a limited test of its idea before we invest in a big campaign.

This is what we mean by adopting an experimental mindset. We're putting our ideas into motion—*execution*—but we're doing it in a way that will allow us to learn. The bonus here is that if we're right, we can begin to see results much sooner than we might otherwise.

The Process of Working with OKRs

Learning is at the heart of successful OKR implementation. So let's take a look at this process. We'll give you an outline here, and then we'll break down each step below.

1. **Review the problem** that you are trying to solve. Remember: Your key result is an outcome and should be written in this form: who + does what + by how much. Your problem lives inside this statement. You're trying to get your "who" to do more or less of something.

2. **Brainstorm solutions** for ways to achieve your key results. In other words, ways that you might get your "who" to "do what."

3. **Decide** what you are going to work on first and how you are going to approach it.

4. **Execute:** Do the work using an experimental, learning-centric, and customer-centric approach.

5. **Measure your results.** OKRs are all about creating results. Whether you're executing or learning, you're trying to make progress and generate results. When you complete a piece of work, you want to measure your results.

6. **Evaluate and learn.** Consider what you've learned from that work. Prepare to start another cycle of learning and execution.

7. **Repeat the process**—executing, measuring, evaluating, and learning—as you work toward your key result.

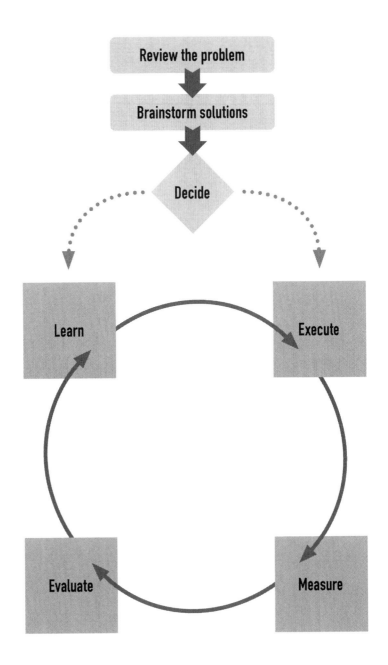

Working Through the Process

Let's look more closely at each part of this process. Keep in mind as you read this that although we're using the word "process" here, we're using it loosely. You can certainly follow these steps, and we think you'll get a lot of value if you do. However, the important ideas to consider here are:

- How you can adopt an experimental mindset
- How you take a more outcome-oriented approach to your work
- How you can be more customer-centric in everything that you do

If you can do those things—regardless of the process—you'll win.

OK, with those big ideas in mind, let's start to look more closely at our execute-and-learn process.

Review Your OKR

This first part of the process is where you orient yourself and your team. Start with your OKR and do everything you can to stay laser-focused on your objective, and especially, on your key results.

For this, you'll want to gather the work that you've done in the process of creating your OKRs. Get your strategy and your OKRs and post them on a wall—or on a virtual whiteboard. Double-check that your key results are written as *who + does what + by how much*. In the next parts of the process, you're going to want to be crystal clear about these elements. If you told stories about your customers or created user journeys, you'll want to keep those close at hand, too.

Why do we do all of this? Well, it's typical for teams that are starting the planning process to list all of the work that they have been asked to do. That's fine. It's important to have a clear picture. It's less common to gather the material that clarifies the reason for the work: the *why*.

So we gather our OKRs and the background material to make the reasons for our work clear.

We also **use our OKRs as a filter**, and we apply that filter to our list of potential work in order to decide what we should work on and what we shouldn't. Remember, OKRs are all about focus. Focusing on your OKR implies that you're *not* going to focus on things that don't drive your OKR. So get your to-do list ready and get ready to have some tough conversations. You're going to need to make some decisions about what you are going to do—and what you're not going to work on right now.

Brainstorm Solutions

Once you've immersed yourself in the objective, it's time to start thinking about how to achieve it. **Your goal at this point is to come up with a list of multiple possible ideas that apply to each key result.** This is a very important point: You don't want to just pick the first idea and run with it. OKRs are all about working your way through multiple ideas and approaches, so you want to take the time to generate options here.

As we discussed above, one approach to this is to look at your to-do lists, project plans, and backlogs of work and to apply your OKR as a filter. You're essentially asking, "Which of these previously planned things do we believe will help us make progress toward our OKR?"

If that's all you do, though, you're missing out on a valuable opportunity, because this is a moment for you to rethink the problem, to get creative, and to come up with new ideas. In other words, this is a moment for you and your team to enter into a creative process.

Coming up with ideas is the work of imagination, invention, and, at its core, design. Figuring out how to solve a problem is inherently a design process. You can make this process as simple as writing a list of all of your ideas and then prioritizing everything on that list. Or you can take a more sophisticated approach, especially if you are a designer or have designers on your team or within your organization. The main thing at this point is to avoid spending too much time at this stage. For now, you're just trying to generate ideas.

The important thing here is that you're creating a list of options. The goal is to write three, six, or perhaps 10 credible ideas, all of which might plausibly help you achieve your outcome.

Hypotheses

It can be helpful to express your ideas as testable hypotheses. This encourages you to approach them in an experimental mindset.

Now, you can use many different templates for hypotheses. The simplest by far is this one:

> *We believe that [making or doing this thing]*
> *Will achieve [this outcome].*

When you write your ideas this way, it connects them back to your outcome, which is important. After all, the whole reason that we're thinking of doing a piece of work is to create an outcome, so writing our ideas this way keeps the idea and the outcome together.

We might write something like this:

> *We believe that running ads in the local newspaper*
> *Will increase foot traffic in our stores by 50%.*

Or even:

> **We believe that doing this:**
> *Running ads in the local newspaper*
>
> **Will achieve our outcome, which is:**
> ***Who:*** *breakfast buyers*
> ***Does what:*** *enter our store*
> ***By how much:*** *increase of 50%.*

In a way, this is the first test of our idea. When we write a hypothesis like this, we can look at it and decide if it makes sense. For example, in the hypothesis above, we don't know if the statement is true, but it seems credible at least and worth trying. Compare that to this one:

> *We believe that running ads in the local paper*
> *Will turn us into millionaires.*

Not credible, right? It's not that running ads is a bad idea, it's just that we have to adjust our expectations about the outcome. So this is what we mean when we say that hypotheses are the first test. They're not the final test, though. To find out if our idea is going to work, we still need to learn more. So let's move on to the next step.

Turning Directives into Hypotheses

Even though OKRs encourage organizations to aim for outcomes and give teams more autonomy in determining the best solutions to work on, some leaders and managers still fall into old habits and give their teams requirements to work on:

> *"Our competitors just launched a subscription service.*
> *We need to do the same."*

> *"I like what I'm hearing about unlimited vacation policies.*
> *I want us to try that out."*

> *"I saw this cool feature on my kid's TikTok. Let's add it to*
> *our banking app."*

Regardless of whether or not these ideas actually make sense for your organization's goals or your team's work, if you're required to execute them, you can still write them as hypotheses in a way that reflects the uncertainty of the real world (and your leaders' lack of omniscience).

Instead of saying, "We *know* we have to make/do this thing," acknowledge the doubt: "We *believe* we have to make/do this thing, and *if* we do it right and it's successful, we *expect* these behavior changes to take place." This sets you up to test the idea and to have a conversation with leadership about those tests and the data that you're about to gather. It helps you have better conversations about these requirements and helps you shift the discussion with your leaders back to outcomes and OKRs.

Decide

At this point in the process, we have a list of ideas: things to work on that we believe will create our key results. Now we have to decide what to do next. There are two important decisions that we need to make at this point.

- First, we need to decide which of our ideas to work on first.
- Then, we need to decide what to do with the ideas that we choose.

Let's look at both of these questions.

What should we work on first?

One of the best ways that we've found to prioritize ideas is to consider them in terms of two questions:

- Which ideas have the most potential to create value?
- And which ideas are the riskiest?

Value may be self-evident, but for the sake of clarity, remember that we're talking about ideas that will most influence customer behavior, as defined in your OKR. Let's go back to our donut store. One key result there was to get more foot traffic to our store. So here, we'd be thinking about which idea is most likely to do just that: increase the number of breakfast buyers who come to our store.

Risk is less obvious, so let's take a minute to consider what we mean here. Usually, risk has to do with unknowns—you're not sure if the idea will work or how long it will take or if your customers will like it or if it's legal or if your marketing department will allow you to do it, or... any one of a million possible unknowns. Fundamentally, these unknowns add up to one simple thing, though: There's some reason to not simply leap head-first into working on the idea.

It turns out that you can map your ideas on a simple chart, and that doing this can help your team decide what to do next. Here's what that chart looks like:

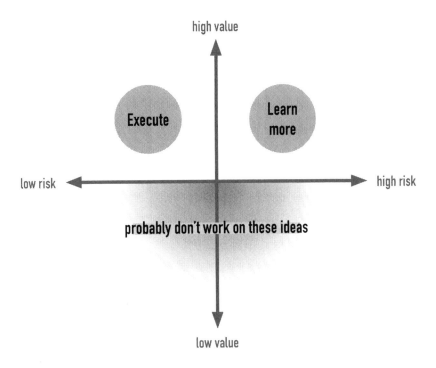

Mapping your ideas this way will help you figure out what to do next.

If your ideas are high value and low risk, your next step should be **Execution**. (See below for a clearer idea of what we mean by that.) If your ideas are risky, we recommend starting with some kind of **Learning Activity**.

One thing to note here: At this point, we're really not sure which ideas are going to be high value and which ones are low value. We need to make our best guess, not get caught up in analysis paralysis, and move forward. If you find yourself arguing with your team about what idea is more valuable, or if you find yourself unable to proceed because you don't want to make the wrong decision, that's a sign that you need more information. In other words, you probably need to do some kind of learning activity before making any more priority decisions. If that's the case, put the ideas in question into the learning bucket and move forward.

Learning Quickly

In many organizations, leaders place a premium on moving quickly. The problem is that "moving quickly" can be code for "let's start executing." In other words, moving quickly doesn't mean "let's do some research."

In fact, we often encounter a distrust of research and other learning activities. We can't count the number of times we've heard leaders say, "Research?!? We don't have time for research!"

Now look, we fundamentally disagree with this idea, even though we admit that there's some truth buried within it. After all, research is fuzzy: How much is enough? When do you stop? When have we learned enough to move forward?

On the other hand, ignoring unknowns is just... well, it's a bad idea. So how do you balance the need to learn with the need to execute quickly?

We like the way Amazon founder Jeff Bezos described his approach to this problem in his 2016 letter to Amazon shareholders:[12]

---

12   https://www.aboutamazon.com/news/company-news/2016-letter-to-shareholders

"Many decisions are reversible, two-way doors. Those decisions can use a lightweight process. For those, so what if you're wrong?

"Second, most decisions should probably be made with somewhere around 70% of the information you wish you had. If you wait for 90%, in most cases, you're probably being slow. Plus, either way, you need to be good at quickly recognizing and correcting bad decisions. If you're good at course correcting, being wrong may be less costly than you think, whereas being slow is going to be expensive for sure."

In other words, look at the decision you need to make, understand what type of decision you're making, and then move quickly to get a *good enough answer for the circumstances.*

What Do We Need to Learn?

The first thing you're going to do is get clarity on what you're trying to learn. Spend some time with your team looking at your idea. Here are some questions you might discuss:

- What's the most important thing for us to learn right now?
- We like this idea, but how might it fail?
- What would we need to learn to feel confident enough to move forward with this idea?
- What might we discover that would make us abandon this idea and move on to the next one?

With your team, make a list of what you'd like to learn.

What's the Best Way to Learn That?

Once you have a list of what you want to learn, the next step is to figure out how you're going to learn it. Sit down with your team and consider your options. Ask yourselves, *What's the fastest way that we can learn enough to make a decision here?*

One option is simple: You can just go talk to people. Remember, in most cases, you're trying to learn about what your customers want and what they need. So having a conversation with them is an incredibly powerful way to learn.

Another fast way to learn directly from your customers is to watch them work. You might even make a simple prototype to show them that will help move the conversation along.

If you've never done any of this, it might feel intimidating, but don't let that stop you. In the back of this book, we've listed some great resources to help get you started.

We've found that teams are often reluctant to talk to customers. They sometimes prefer to use surveys instead. Surveys are appealing because they promise statistical significance—and you don't need to talk to anyone face-to-face.

Here's our advice: Avoid surveys. They're hard to do well, and you won't learn nearly as much as you will from in-person conversations. You'll learn more from talking to six customers than you will from surveying 100. Trust us here.

When You Need Numbers

There are times when you will need numbers, of course. How big is the market? How many people feel this way? What are our customers actually doing with our products? Sometimes your learning activities and research need to be quantitative. In these cases, we recommend reaching out to a data analyst or researcher to help you get these numbers. Work with them to explain your problem and your learning goals.

Also, explain what's riding on your decision. Researching a life-or-death question is very different from researching the color choices you're making for your office furniture. Consider what's at stake, so you can choose the right method of gathering data.

Execution, With an Experimental Mindset

This next part of the process—*execution*—is, for most of us, the most familiar. Our jobs all consist of some core responsibilities, and this is where we'll execute them. But if you've come this far with us on this OKR journey, you know that things are going to change.

Execution for Outputs vs. Execution to Create Outcomes

Most companies manage work in terms of outputs: the things that people make or the things that they deliver. If you are a software developer, your work might be organized around creating and delivering software features. If you're in HR, your work might be organized around creating and delivering a new corporate training.

These things remain important when working with OKRs, of course, but we want to think of them as means to an end—an outcome. When we deliver that feature for example, what will our customers be doing differently? When we deliver that training, what will our trainees be doing differently?

With OKRs, we're always focused on creating outcomes. That means that we want to avoid spending a quarter working on a deliverable, only to discover that it doesn't create value. Instead, we want to structure our work to help us learn.

This can mean working in smaller increments: Could we make a smaller version of that feature or that training—one that takes only a month to get into our customers' hands? Then we could measure to see if the feature is creating new customer behaviors. This would give us two or three attempts in each quarter to create our outcomes.

It might also mean structuring our work to look for leading indicators. For example, instead of waiting until the end of a three-month training program to see if it's valuable, we might plan to measure leading indicators. Are people registering for the training? Are they showing up for training sessions? Are they using what they're learning after each class? Are they recommending the training to their peers?

Execution for Learning

Sometimes, the best way to test your ideas is to put them into action. As we discussed above, the big challenge with OKRs is that we're never sure if ideas are going to work—if they'll create the key results that we're seeking. We can learn a lot by talking to people, watching them work, and prototyping. But sometimes, you need to make something, put it into the world, and see what happens.

This idea has gained a lot of popularity in recent years, especially in the tech startup world. People learned to make *minimum viable products*—small and simple experiments, designed to test their ideas. This technique (making the smallest possible piece of something, just enough to let you learn something) is one of the most powerful ways to test risky ideas. Experiments, after all, are the way that science tests risky ideas—and does so in ways that are safe to fail—in a test tube or lab or some other controlled way. We can take inspiration from this way of learning and try it in our work, too.

Experiments are useful when you have an idea that feels very risky. When this is the case, sit down as a team and discuss:

- What's the biggest risk here?
- What do we need to learn first to mitigate this risk?
- Is there something that we might make
  to help us learn about this risk?

For instance, instead of rolling out a whole new training program for all 1,000 people in your corporation, test it with just 15 people and then scale it up from there.

The Real Trick: Doing Both at the Same Time

Of course, it's possible to deliver value and to learn at the same time. Structuring your work so that you can do both is the ultimate objective of working with OKRs.

Think of experiments as a different way of framing the work you're doing—to focus it more specifically. This reframing is important because learning *is* work and execution *is* work—and we want to do both at the same time.

Let's say, for example, that shipping for your retail operation has been backed up for months, and you need to find a way to get the product out the door much faster. Your hypothesis is that if you change the layout of the warehouse, the popular products will be easier to find and faster to package. The risk, however, is that changing the entire warehouse's layout causes massive disruption for employees and shipping processes across the company without the guarantee that it will work. So, instead of your job being to "change the layout of the warehouse to make shipping more efficient," your experiment can narrow the scope: "We're going to change the layout of the *sneaker department's* warehouse to make shipping more efficient." You're not tackling the whole enchilada—just taking one bite.

In this example, you are actually beginning to implement your idea, just not at scale. At the same time, you're looking for evidence that says the warehouse redesign will change staff behavior before deploying it broadly. If it fails, you've impacted only the sneaker department. At the same time, if it works, you're creating value in the sneaker department and now know what needs to be done throughout the operation. So you're both learning *and* executing.

Measure

Every part of the OKR Cycle that we've described so far is in service of achieving your key results. So as you work, you want to measure how much closer to—or farther away from—your target metrics you're getting. You want to be able to assess whether you're doing the right things or whether you need to change gears.

Measuring your progress requires two main things:

1. collecting data at every stage of your work
2. sharing that data and ensuring it's accessible organization-wide.

Collecting Data

There are two different kinds of data that we gather: quantitative and qualitative. Here's how they break down:

Quantitative data = numbers

These are the measurements of customer behavior, often gathered through analytics tools, that tell you what is happening and how well you're progressing. Using the frame of "[who] [does what] [by how much]," this is the "does what" and "by how much."

Qualitative data = words (and things you can't count)

This is what you get from your interactions with your customers. This tells you why what's happening is happening: why people are doing what they're doing and why you're making progress or not. Qualitative data helps explain the numbers and can also help you figure out what adjustments you might want to make to your work.

You need to collect and share both quantitative and qualitative data throughout your organization.

Collecting and sharing data sounds pretty straightforward, at least in theory. You do an activity, track the responses you get, store that information, and share it widely. And yet in many organizations, it's not that simple. There are a few reasons for that. Oftentimes organizations will track quantitative data but not qualitative. Or they'll track the metrics they see at the end of a project but not what they see along the way.

Or they'll collect data but limit who can see it and when. Or they'll collect the wrong data—data on system performance, rather than on customer behavior.

No matter which version of the story it is, if organizations don't collect and share both quantitative and qualitative data at every stage of their work, there's only so much their teams will be able to understand and accomplish. Simply put: Without data, you're going to have problems.

For instance, let's say you run a small floral business and you notice that the number of subscribers to your weekly flower delivery service has stagnated. This observation is based on your quantitative data—your numbers. As you look more deeply, you realize that a few of your most loyal customers haven't renewed their subscriptions.

What should you do? The data doesn't tell us, so we need to plan some learning activities to get the qualitative data that will help us understand the numbers. In other words, we probably want to go talk to people.

What Data Is Important?

For quantitative data, pay particular attention to data about customer behavior: visitors to your website, purchases of your newest product line, email bounces, new subscribers, failed shipments, survey respondents, and so on. Count every customer behavior you can with whatever analytics systems, measurement tools, and programs you've got.

For qualitative data, conduct customer research. Talk to people, watch them in action, and ask them to fill you in on why they do what they do. Store their answers in an easy-to-use and easy-to-update system.

Choosing the Right Key Result, Even if You Can't Measure It

There are times when you may choose metrics for your key results that your team or organization doesn't currently measure or that are difficult to measure. For example, let's say your team decides you need to measure foot traffic in your retail store, but you don't currently measure that in any way. What should you do?

It's tempting to throw up your hands and say, "Well, I guess we can't use that metric for our key result. Better pick something else." But that's not always the case.

Just because you don't currently have the measurement tool you need doesn't mean you shouldn't choose the metric as a key result. If it's the metric that makes the most sense for achieving your goals—and it's something your organization should find a way to measure anyway for its long-term success—then it's worth figuring out a way to measure it.

It may take you six months to build the system that measures what you need. It may mean convincing the people with the purse strings to purchase an expensive tool that will allow you to get the measurement. It may mean you need to use a proxy metric or measurement process in the meantime.

For instance, in a retail store, you might ask employees to manually count every customer who walks into the store at two different, specific time periods throughout the day so you can extrapolate the numbers to get a better estimate of total foot traffic. Regardless of whether and how you need to adapt your expectations and data collection methods, don't get disheartened. If it's the right metric, you should use it.

Evaluate and Reflect

At this point, you've done the work and you've collected data about it. You're now in a position to evaluate the work. Did it create the key result that you wanted?

When we're working with OKRs, we use check-in meetings as the occasions for these conversations. We meet with our teams on a regular basis to evaluate and reflect—doing this weekly, monthly, quarterly, and annually.

In the next chapter, we'll go into check-in meetings in detail and discuss how teams can evaluate, reflect, and adjust course in these meetings.

Repeat

The final piece of the executing and learning loop is that you repeat it. That's what makes it a loop. You'll need to determine the right rhythm is for you and your team: You might be very strict about your executing and learning loops and use a two-week "sprint" to structure your time. Or you might take a looser approach to structuring your time. After all, the OKR Cycle has built-in checkpoints to structure your time. (We'll talk about that more in the next chapter.)

The important idea here is that executing and learning are continuous: You want to do them both continuously and, to the greatest extent possible, keep both kinds of work in motion at all times. In other words, avoid long phases of learning or protracted stretches of execution. Use timeboxes to move quickly from execution to learning, using the data you collect along the way to create value quickly.

Key Takeaways

1. Working with OKRs requires an experimental mindset. Because OKRs don't specify solutions, using them means that we need to figure out what to work on to achieve our goals. The best way to do this is by adopting an experimental mindset toward our work.

2. To help us achieve our goals, we embrace research and other learning activities. We want to balance learning and execution, avoiding both prolonged periods of study but also avoiding execution without learning and reflection.

3. We collect two kinds of data in order to learn. Quantitative data are the numbers—the measurements of customer behavior, gathered largely through analytics tools, that tell you *what* is happening and how well you're progressing. Qualitative data is the information you learn from customer research that tells you *why* what's happening is happening—why you're making progress or not.

Chapter 11

Checking In

Organizations that use OKRs hold check-in meetings regularly to review their progress. These meetings are critical moments for teams and the broader organization, and are the final major component of the OKR Cycle. In this chapter, we'll cover check-ins in detail.

Why Check In?

It's nearing the end of Q1, and the tax filing deadline in the United States is approaching. The marketing team at FastTax has been working on improving email-open rates and click-through rates. Those are their key results for the quarter. The hope is that if more people open the company's marketing emails and click through to the website, more people will file their taxes through FastTax. That's the organization's key result.

So far, the marketing numbers have been good. Email-open rates have gone up an average of 8%, and click-through rates have nearly doubled. Sounds like success, doesn't it? Not so fast. Though the marketing key results have gone up, there's little progress on the ultimate goal: There hasn't been any increase in the number of people signing up for FastTax. What gives?

This situation is exactly the point of the check-in meeting.

Check-ins are regular meetings where you meet with your team, look at the data to understand the results of your work, line up that data with your current activities to see if you can understand what's causing what, and then decide what to work on next. Frequent and transparent check-ins are one of the most important parts of OKRs and critical to your success in using them.

There's more to check-ins than simply figuring out what to do next. Check-ins also create many of the benefits of using OKRs.

1. They create **alignment** between and among teams.
2. They create **transparency** for better decision-making.
3. They ensure **agility** in the system so that you can change course quickly.

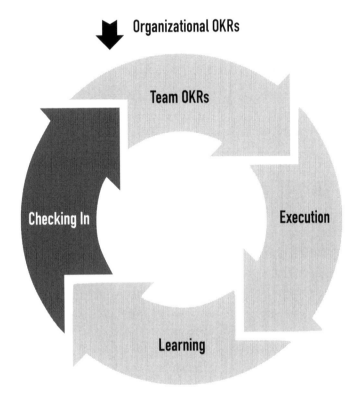

The Rhythm of Check-in Meetings

To get the benefits of check-ins, **you need consistency and predictability in your check-ins.**

There are three kinds of OKR check-in meetings that we consider to be required: weekly, monthly, and quarterly.

- The **weekly check-in meeting** is a pulse check, used to quickly monitor progress and how the team is feeling about that progress. This check-in is very important but may not need to be its own meeting. Some teams that already hold weekly meetings can simply add the weekly OKR check-in to their existing meeting agenda. Attendees for this meeting can be made up of the team responsible for the OKR.
- **The monthly check-in meeting** is for teams to review their progress and make decisions about what to work on next. This is typically a meeting of the immediate team and supervisor. This is where the marketing team would talk about their work to improve email-open and click-through rates. They'd review their progress, examine their tactics, talk about what they've done and what they've learned, and decide what to work on in the coming month. They'd share all of this with the larger stakeholder group after the meeting.
- The **quarterly check-in meeting** is for teams and their leaders to determine if they've hit their OKRs and if they should set new ones or keep working toward the ones they've had. This meeting is usually attended by a larger group, including more senior leaders and peer teams. The focus is on the bigger question: How are each team's results contributing to the larger goals of the organization?

In addition to those meetings, teams sometimes add a fourth meeting to the mix: the retrospective. You should definitely hold retrospective meetings, but if you're already doing so, you might simply incorporate this topic into your existing meeting.

- **The retrospective meeting** is used to talk about and improve the working process and the process of using OKRs. If your team is already holding regular retrospective meetings, you don't need to create another one—but you should add some OKR-related material to the meeting.

What's the Right Rhythm?

Most organizations start with monthly and quarterly meetings. That rhythm isn't magic, sacred, or immutable. If your business runs on a faster or slower cycle, you can adjust your meeting rhythm to something that makes sense for you. Our recommendation, though, is to start with monthly and quarterly meetings unless you have a good reason to change. If you do change, keep in mind that you want your cycles to be as short as possible.

Finally, keep in mind that these monthly and quarterly meetings are the formal rituals of the OKR Cycle. These meetings are required if you want to make OKRs work. You want to make the time in your schedule to hold these meetings and to dedicate the time to the topic.

The other meetings that we mentioned—weekly and retrospective meetings—are important but can be added to the agendas of your existing meetings. Your weekly OKR meeting could be part of your weekly planning meeting. It might not even have to be a meeting; it could be a group-chat message. The point here is that everyone on the team has a responsibility to proactively share updates and be radically transparent so you're all always operating and making decisions with the most up-to-date information. These little check-ins should include your leaders, too. You don't want your monthly check-in to be the first they're hearing about how your work is going.

Similarly, you want to check in on your OKR process at least monthly. If you're not currently holding monthly retrospective meetings, you should add that to your process. If you are, then you can simply add OKR-related questions to the agenda of that meeting.

Assessing Your Progress

We use check-in meetings to review our progress. So let's consider how we do that.

OKRs ask us to measure our progress on a regular basis for a number of reasons. We do this in order to focus our work. We do this in order to hold ourselves accountable for results. And we do this in terms of customer behavior because we're using the tool to become more customer-centric. All of this is in the service of achieving an important goal for the company. So it makes sense then that when we check in, we should always be looking at our measure of progress.

Your Primary Measure of Progress: Outcomes

When we use OKRs, our **primary measure of progress** is customer behavior—the outcomes that we selected when we wrote our key results. We always want to be tracking whether or not our work is influencing customer behavior. So in our check-in meetings, we begin there. We review our key results and then look at the data. Did the work that we did over the last week, month, or quarter cause any change in customer behavior?

As we said in Chapter 9, this means that we need to structure our work so that it continuously generates outcomes. In a pre-OKR world, we might have decided to build software for six months, hoping that, once launched, it would change customer behavior. With OKRs, though, we change the way we work so that we can deliver value to customers continuously—and then see the results of that work continuously changing as well.

A Secondary Progress Assessment: Confidence

OKRs also have secondary ways of assessing your progress. Secondary assessments don't actually measure the value that we've created. They can be important, though, as a way of managing our work toward that goal.

Many teams like to use **confidence** as a secondary assessment. This can be particularly useful during check-ins. Confidence is pretty simple—it's an unscientific expression of how you're feeling about your progress. The best way to use confidence is to use it to start a discussion with your team, using the question, *How confident are you that we're going to achieve our result?* You can use any scale you like—some teams use a quick vote, holding up zero to five fingers to indicate their confidence level. Others use high-medium-low. The point is that this question is a *conversation starter*, not a measurement tool. The goal is to identify issues early so that the team can decide if some action is needed. By itself, confidence is not that useful as a measure for non-team communication. The conversations that you'll have may surface important issues, though—those issues can be included in external communications.

In other words, don't use confidence as a measure of progress. Use it to have good conversations about your actual progress.

Another Secondary Progress Assessment: Scoring

Earlier in the book, we talked about scoring OKRs. When you defined your OKRs, you may have created a grading scale so that you could evaluate your progress. For example, let's say that your goal was to increase foot traffic to your retail store by 100% this quarter. At your check-in meeting, you review the numbers and see that you've grown foot traffic, but only by 50%. Is that good? Is that bad? Should you continue to work on that OKR? Should you revise it? Should you abandon it?

Scoring gives you a tool to help you answer those questions because you've discussed them in advance. We think scoring is most useful at quarterly check-ins once you've had a chance to see some results and review the trending data.

One thing to keep in mind, though, is that "scoring" is a secondary assessment. When all is said and done, it's not the scores that matter—it's the results. For this reason, many teams and organizations choose to skip scoring and to focus their energy and attention on tracking the results directly without adding the additional overhead of scoring.

How to Run a Check-in Meeting

All check-in meetings use the same basic flow, which looks like this:

- Opening: Review progress
- Middle: Learning, opportunities, obstacles
- Closing: Set next steps

In each type of check-in meeting, we conduct that business a little differently. In the weekly meeting, the premium is on efficient use of time, so we try to cover our topics quickly, identifying only things that need immediate action and correction. In the monthly meeting, we give ourselves more time to assess our results. In the quarterly meeting, we zoom out to more strategic concerns. Let's look at each of these meetings by looking at some agendas that you can use and adapt for your own meetings.

The "No Surprises" Rule

One important goal of OKRs is to promote transparency. In practice, we try to use OKRs and the OKR process to create this transparency. One way that we do this is with our check-in meetings. We meet weekly, monthly, and quarterly. We report and discuss what we're seeing each week, so that big issues don't show up for the first time in monthly or quarterly meetings.

As you're holding your check-in meetings, pay attention to the things you think that your team and stakeholders need to know, and raise those issues early. Communicate them as broadly as you think it appropriate after the meeting. Make sure that these meetings really drive transparency. If you're doing this well, the check-in meeting will focus on the future rather than what's happened in the past. Ideally everyone is coming to the meeting aware of what's already transpired and excited about deciding next steps.

The Weekly Check-in Meeting

The weekly check-in meeting is your opportunity to stay aligned with your immediate team. This meeting isn't for stakeholders—though you can communicate a summary to them. It's also not a problem-solving meeting. It is intended to be a status meeting that creates transparency and clarity. It's your weekly opportunity to share learnings and to catch issues before they turn into big ones. Schedule 30 minutes for this meeting.

One key to this meeting is facilitation. Someone should run the meeting, and that person should be aggressive about timekeeping. You may either rotate this responsibility or make it a standing role. In addition to a facilitator, you should identify a person who will be responsible for capturing and sharing notes from this meeting.

One way to keep this meeting efficient is to remember that this isn't a problem-solving meeting. Instead, you're capturing a list of topics and issues that require further work—and require follow-up sessions. Keep things moving, otherwise these weekly check-ins will start to turn into long, draining sessions, and people will be less and less inclined to attend and to take the meeting seriously.

Who: *immediate team only*

Opening: *10 minutes*

- **Share the data.**
  Review the key results that you've generated so far. Your expectations should be that you're moving these numbers every week. (This may not be true or possible in every case, but this should be your default assumption.)
- **Work-in-progress highlights.** The team highlights anything that they're working on that meets at least one of these criteria:
  - Is related to the OKR
  - Is going exceptionally well or exceptionally badly
  - Requires some attention from the team
- **Confidence review.**
  Ask the team, "How confident are each of you that we'll achieve our goal?" Take a quick vote, using a 0 to 5 scale, by holding up the fingers on one hand. Ask people to share why they voted the way that they did. (Keep it brief!) Then identify any issues that come up from the discussion.

Middle: *10 minutes*

- **Learnings, issues, obstacles, and opportunities.**
  Discuss any issues that you identified in the
  confidence review. Raise any obstacles or
  blockers. Highlight any new opportunities.
  Highlight any major new learning. Keep in
  mind that you have only 10 minutes here, so
  the goal of this discussion is to raise topics
  that you might require further follow-up.

Closing: *10 minutes*

- **Next steps.**
  Review the list of issues, obstacles, and
  opportunities. Decide on next steps. If the next
  step isn't clear, then plan a follow-up work session
  for the appropriate subset of the team to work on
  the topic. Finally, decide on owners. If the item
  doesn't have an owner, it probably won't get done.

After the meeting.

- **Capture the key points from the meeting
  and share.** At a minimum, it's important to
  keep an internal record for the team, but
  it's a good idea to share some version of
  the meeting with stakeholders as well.

The Monthly Check-in Meeting

The **monthly check-in meeting** is intended to be a broader review of your progress. This is a meeting at which stakeholders are welcome and expected to attend. Schedule more time for this because you want to have more in-depth discussions with stakeholders while you have the time. Plan to schedule 60 to 90 minutes for this meeting.

Your agenda for the monthly meeting can and should include many of the topics from the weekly meeting.

Who: *The immediate team plus stakeholders*

Opening:

- **Share the data.**
- **Work-in-progress review.**
- *Optional:* **Confidence review.**
  This is a high-trust activity. You'll have to decide for yourself if you feel comfortable confidence voting with stakeholders in the room. If you don't think people will be open and honest while stakeholders are present, then skip this activity.
- **Stakeholder context updates.**
  It's important for the team to get strategic guidance from stakeholders. This is a great moment for that. After you've shared the results, before you move on to discussion, ask your stakeholders to share any significant updates that will be important for your team, your OKRs, and the work that you'll be doing in the coming months.

Middle:

- **Learnings, issues, obstacles, and opportunities.**
  Plan to focus this discussion on what you've
  learned in the month since your last meeting.
  Really lean into this part. This is your opportunity
  to demonstrate your expertise as a learning
  team. It's also foundational for dealing with
  the next topic: obstacles and opportunities.
- **Obstacles:**
  If you've done a good job sharing your learnings,
  the discussion of obstacles and opportunities
  should flow naturally from there. This is the
  moment when the conversation begins to turn
  to what's next, so, as much as possible, use
  the evidence and learnings that you've just
  presented as the foundation of this discussion.
- **OKR Confirmation:**
  Confirm or adjust your OKRs.
  - Under normal circumstances, you don't
    want to make big changes to your OKRs on
    a monthly basis. That said, you *do* want to
    confirm that the OKRs that you've set are the
    right targets for the team. Have an explicit
    conversation with stakeholders. Given
    the strategic landscape, are these still the
    right objectives? And, given our progress,
    are these still the key results that we're
    aiming for? Should we adjust up or down?

- It's OK if you adjust your key results in response to your learning and progress. However, if you find yourself tinkering with your key results every month or making big changes—especially changing your objectives every month—you probably have a problem that you need to deal with. (This is a topic for your retrospective meeting, which we'll cover below.)

Closing:

- **Next Steps**
  As with your weekly meetings, try to avoid problem-solving in this meeting as much as possible. Decide next steps, even if that means putting off thorny questions for a follow-up meeting. Assign owners. Don't be afraid to ask stakeholders to own issues that they should own. If you've done a good job presenting your learnings, it should be clear to everyone where and how stakeholders can step up.

After the meeting.

- Capture the key points from the meeting and share.

The Quarterly Check-in Meeting

The **quarterly check-in meeting** is a kind of "all of the above" meeting, with a specific emphasis on re-confirming, adjusting, or changing the team's OKRs. It's a major milestone. This meeting is often focused at the workgroup level—in other words, in addition to your team, it can include your peer teams. The idea is that if a group of teams are working on related or coordinated OKRs, you probably want to evaluate your progress together and you definitely want to coordinate any changes to the OKRs of the group.

In terms of agenda, you can use the monthly check-in meeting agenda, with revisions as needed if you have gathered multiple teams. Within that agenda though, we suggest emphasizing the following topics:

- **Review the data:**
  Make sure your quarterly meeting is grounded in good data. You really want to focus on your primary data—results. This is a moment to bring in the scoring rubric that you created when you wrote your key results (see Chapter 6).
- **Stakeholder context:**
  Three months is a long time for most organizations. What's changed? What is the organization still committed to? This will be important for any adjustments that you make.
- **Learnings:**
  This is a critical opportunity for teams to share what they've learned. Make sure that you're ready to share your most important learnings.
- **OKR confirmation:**
  The quarterly meeting is where most organizations welcome adjustments to their OKRs. Leave time for this conversation. You may need a breakout session to write your new OKRs, but this meeting is the time to decide whether changes are needed and, broadly speaking, what those changes should be.

Mid-Cadence Upsets

As we said, those are the typical, "set" cadences for check-ins. But if something significant happens to your business, your industry, or the world (a global pandemic, anyone?), *don't be afraid to pull the ripcord and change course mid-cadence.*

The standard cyclical timelines are for business as usual. When major and unexpected events enter the picture, that's no longer "business as usual," and you shouldn't wait until your next scheduled meeting to figure out how the events affect your OKRs and the work you're doing to achieve them. You really don't want to reach the point where your leaders ask, "Why didn't you tell me about this two weeks ago?"

Because OKRs require you to collect, track, and act on the data you're collecting at all times, they're agile by design. Take advantage of that agility when the situation calls for it.

Revising Your OKRs

Assess Your Progress Toward "Done"

One of the trickier judgment calls in the OKR world is determining whether or not you've made enough progress to move on, or if you should keep working on your OKR.

This is where your OKR scoring conversations can be helpful. In Chapter 6, we suggested that when you write your key results, you consider three possible scores for each result: We Delivered, We Fell Short, and We Failed to Deliver. This is the moment when you want to pull out that scoring sheet and use it to guide your discussion.

The thing to keep in mind is that key results are not necessarily meant to be absolute goals. Unless you have a regulation to follow, you don't need to hit 100% of your target metrics for your efforts to be a success. **Hitting 70 to 80% of the metrics is quite successful, and in many cases, it's not worth it to keep going for 100%.** (It's often unattainable anyway.) If, for instance, you're fixating on one customer behavior, don't try to squeeze everything out of it. The longer you squeeze, the less you get.

You can think of it like reading a thermometer versus a barometer. A thermometer just tells you what the temperature is; a barometer, on the other hand, tells you the atmospheric pressure, which can help forecast weather patterns. So, if you track the change in barometric readings over time, you can predict when it's going to rain by seeing if the pressure is trending up. You can do something similar with your key result metrics. Look at the rate of change in your metrics versus the effort you're putting in. The rate of return on your efforts is likely to decrease the longer you test one tactic, so if you see that the rate of behavior change is slowing down but you're still putting in a lot of effort, try something new. These check-in meetings are where you make those assessments and figure out what that something new should be.

How to Revise Your Key Results

So, let's say that you've come to the conclusion that you need to revise your OKRs, either by creating a new objective, or by keeping the objective, but adjusting the key results. That's OK! **If the data you've collected over the course of your work leads you to this conclusion, then this is actually a good thing. In these cases, this is an example of the organizational agility that we use OKRs to create.** In changing course, you reduce the amount of effort sunk into the wrong effort and start working on things that are hopefully more effective. But before you set new OKRs, you'll need to have a conversation with your stakeholders.

Have the Conversation with Your Stakeholders

Whether this conversation happens at a scheduled monthly or quarterly meeting or you feel the need to have the conversation in the middle of a cycle, approaching your stakeholders about changing your OKRs can be a daunting, if not terrifying, conversation. In all likelihood, someone (likely your stakeholder) is on the hook for the goals your team committed to. It's crucial that you root the conversation in evidence, otherwise there's a risk your team will simply seem uninterested in working hard to move a particular result forward.

To maximize the chances of success, approach the conversation in the following ways:

- **It should never be a surprise.**
  The onus is on you and your team to continuously share learnings, decisions, and risks with your stakeholders. When it's time to have "the conversation," you'll have a lengthy paper trail to justify your request.
- **Bring the proof.**
  Even if you dependably shared your concerns with your leadership team ahead of the meeting, don't bet on them having read them. Always come prepared with a well-designed presentation of the data that backs up your request to change goals. If you show up with evidence of your experiments, customer testimonials, and data that shows that, any way you slice it, your customers will not significantly shift their behavior to achieve your desired key result, you'll stand a much better chance of convincing your stakeholders that changing your goals is the right move.
- **Come in with an opinion.**
  We hate the mantra "Don't bring me problems, bring me solutions." It discourages teams from bringing up issues if they don't know how to solve them. That said, in this situation, you're the ones closest to the data. You're the ones working on it every day. You should at least have an opinion and suggestion about how to reset your OKRs and what to do next. Write out the reasoning behind your argument and list the behaviors you believe you should target instead.

- **Be prepared to explain the cost of not changing course.**
  These conversations won't always go your way. What happens then? Know the cost (in time, budget, etc.) already sunk into the work, how much more is potentially at risk and, perhaps most importantly, what won't get done if you maintain the current trajectory. If stakeholders are on the fence, use this information to try to tip the balance.

The Retrospective Meeting

Retrospective, or retro, meetings are a type of meeting that teams use to look at the work of the past period with an eye toward improvement. Teams typically ask questions like, *What went well? What didn't go so well? What would we like to change?* Retro meetings are important opportunities for reflection.

What's the difference between a retro meeting and a check-in? Well, check-ins are focused on the work and on the results. Retros are focused on the process. It's an opportunity to look at the *way we're working* and to try to improve that.

There's a lot of material out there on retrospective meetings, and we want to keep this book short, so we'll just offer one starting point here, and encourage you to explore other sources to learn more about retro meetings.

One note: If you've never held a retro meeting before, try to find an experienced facilitator to run your first. Psychological safety is important in retros, and it's easy even for well-intentioned people to mess that up. You'll increase your team's chance of success if you work with someone who's done this before.

A Typical Retro Meeting

In a typical retro meeting, you begin by asking everyone in the meeting to work individually, writing down on sticky notes (or the digital equivalent) their observations of the past period. Usually, the meeting facilitator will provide a set of questions for people to respond to. The most common questions are these:

1. In the past period, what went well?
2. What do I have questions about?
3. What went badly?

After everyone has written their notes, people share them, usually posting them to a wall or shared workspace. Then, the facilitator leads discussion about the topics that people have raised.

Once the topics have been discussed, the team can pick a small number of issues to improve, decide what to do about them, assign owners, and close the meeting. Your next retro meeting should open with a report on progress made against those issues.

Use the Principles

In addition to the questions above, for OKR retrospectives, we like to use the OKR principles that we shared at the start of this book to help guide the meeting.

The key principles of OKRs are

1. Focus
2. Autonomy
3. Alignment
4. Accountability
5. Transparency
6. Agility
7. Customer-centricity

We suggest starting by posting those principles on the wall or in the shared workspace. Then, as you're considering the questions (what went well, what do I have questions about, what went badly?), consider them in terms of each principle. For example, you might ask yourself, *What did we do that increased our focus? What did we do that made it harder to focus?*

The goal of using OKRs is to increase these things. Your retro meeting should help you discover where, when, and how you're making progress toward these goals.

Key Takeaways

1. OKRs are assumptions, so it's likely that yours may be wrong. Check-ins are regular meetings that help you mitigate the risks of your assumptions. They are where you analyze what's working and what's not and determine if and what you need to change to see more progress.
2. There are three different types of check-ins:
    a. **weekly check-ins** for your team to stay in sync, monitor progress, and make day-to-day decisions about tactics
    b. **monthly check-ins** for your team and your supervisor to assess your progress and make decisions about your next steps for the month ahead
    c. **quarterly check-ins with leadership** to determine if you've hit your OKRs and what you should focus on in the next quarter.
3. If your experiments don't achieve your objective, you need to determine which piece was wrong: the solution you tested, a variable of the solution, or the key result that you set initially. To do this, talk to your customers first, then test more variables.
4. If the data overwhelmingly challenges the validity of either your objective, your key results, or both, then you must change them. This is the organizational agility OKRs enable. Bring the proof to your stakeholders, along with an opinion about what to do next. You will need their sign-off to change your OKRs.

Chapter 12

Planning with OKRs

The last piece of the OKR Cycle is making and communicating our plans.

We've said before that OKRs are a way of working that changes how we approach our work. Instead of only planning the stuff that we make (outputs), we plan to create results (outcomes). Communicating these kinds of plans requires some new planning tools and new planning methods.

So how do we plan our work when we're not sure what work will be effective? And how do we communicate our plans when our plans are now subject to change?

The main approach that we want to encourage here is to embrace the uncertainty and encourage agility.

How? The short answer is that we're going to approach planning like this:

1. Plan in short cycles with a high tolerance for ambiguity and an appetite for course correction.
2. Filter your to-do list and any inbound work requests through your OKRs.
3. Communicate your plans with an outcome-based roadmap that is driven by key results.

In this chapter, we're going to walk you through all three of these steps. We'll also talk about how to handle work that doesn't fit neatly into this framework, notably date-driven work with hard deadlines.

Embrace Uncertainty. Encourage Agility.

We make plans for many reasons. For one thing, thinking about the future and how to handle its complexity can be overwhelming. Making a nice crisp plan helps. And it feels good, too. The problem is that plans are brittle—they rarely unfold perfectly. The formulation attributed to Dwight D. Eisenhower is on point here: *Planning is essential, but plans are useless.*

To quote another great fighter, "Everyone has a plan 'til they get punched in the mouth."[13]

What we want then are plans that are not brittle, are not useless, and that help us recover when things go wrong. This is why we want to embrace uncertainty and encourage agility. It will help us stay focused on our goal—creating outcomes for our customers—as events unfold in ways that we didn't predict.

Plan in Short Cycles

The first tactic here is to **reduce the time horizon of your plans.** With OKRs, you're no longer planning a full year's worth of work. Rather, you're planning for one OKR cycle—in most cases, one quarter—at a time.

Drafting detailed plans that stretch many months into the future is a fool's errand. You can do it, by all means, but know that anything you plan for more than one to two quarters out relies on guesswork. It sets false expectations for both your teams and your leaders. **Reduce the time horizon of your plans.**

13　It's unclear if Mike Tyson ever actually said this, and there's some debate about the Eisenhower quote too, and yes, our strategic Prussian friend Von Moltke is in here too, but these quotes serve to communicate the ideas and we like them so we're using them.

In autumn, 2008, Jeff got a new job at a company called The Ladders, which was a job-search engine for people who made $100,000 or more a year. Job boards are like dating sites: They need a balanced ecosystem of job-seekers and open positions to operate as they're supposed to. As you may remember, autumn 2008 was a bad time for jobs. Within three weeks of Jeff starting at The Ladders, the financial crisis began, and The Ladders' balanced ecosystem of open positions to job-seekers turned upside-down overnight. His team had a product roadmap built out nine months into the future. What were they going to do now? Stick their heads in the sand and follow the plan, or change the plan so they could respond to their drastically changed environment?

Now, this is an extreme example. Events like those of 2008 don't happen all the time. But smaller and similarly unexpected changes do happen all the time. By acknowledging the limits of what you can know and predict, you reduce the risk of committing to ideas that don't work. What's more, this acknowledgment encourages you to measure your results and deploy people and resources in directions that are having the most success.

Filter Your To-do List with Your OKRs

When organizations start using OKRs, people (teams, leaders, everyone) tend to wonder what will happen to the work they've been doing and the projects they're in the middle of. Nobody wants to "waste" any work they've already done, so there's a temptation to reverse engineer the current to-do list to fit the new goals.

But imagine that you were in Chicago and driving east to New York City. You're making good time, but suddenly you get a call—you need to go to California instead! You wouldn't keep driving east would you? No, you'd turn the car around and start heading west.

In that spirit, once you've set new goals, it's important to reevaluate whether or not you're working on the right things. This doesn't mean you need to throw out your previous to-do list entirely. It does mean evaluating the items on your list through the lens of your new goals in order to decide what still makes sense to work on and what doesn't.

The best time to review your plan is after your team's check-in meetings. Remember, check-in meetings are not planning meetings, but you're going to be making decisions in those meetings that will impact your plans. That means you are going to want to follow your check-ins with planning meetings.

To filter your work with OKRs, gather all of your to-do lists, plans, backlogs, commitments, etc. Then, create four lists:

- A *Keep Doing* list
- A *Maybe* list
- A *Stop Doing* list
- A *Start Doing* list

Then, for every existing work item, ask: *Will this activity help us achieve one of our key results?*

- If the answer is "yes," add the item to a *Keep Doing* list.
- If the answer is "maybe," add it to a *Maybe* list.
- If the answer is "no," add the item to a *Stop Doing* list.

Here's a diagram we use to help teams visualize this:

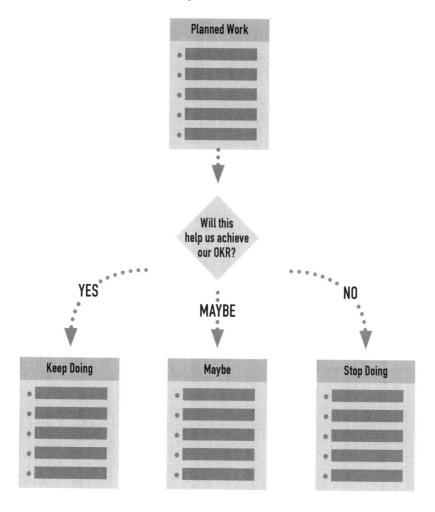

If an idea or activity no longer makes sense, put it in the *Stop Doing* list to filter it out completely—regardless of how far along you are in its development. Remember, sunk cost is lost. You can't get it back, and continuing to invest time and/or money in ideas that will no longer help you achieve your goals is pointless. Some teams find it helpful to keep a list of projects like this. You can call it an archive or cold-storage or a morgue. Just put it away.

One thing to keep in mind here is that this process—as simple as it seems—is really difficult. The hard part isn't filtering the list. The hard part is saying "no" to work, especially to work in progress. After all, you've been doing that work because someone thought doing it was a good idea. Maybe you and the team decided to do it. Maybe someone requested it. Maybe you've made commitments. All of this puts pressure on your decision-making progress.

One thing that can make this a little easier is to soften the Stop Doing list by turning it into a Not Now list. You might want to kill the work entirely but putting it in the Not Now list can relieve some of the organizational pressure to continue the work. After all, things that make the Stop Doing list aren't necessarily bad ideas; they just aren't the best ideas for right now. It's possible that these rejected items will find their way back onto the list of things to work on in the future. (It might, on the other hand, create a false expectation, so be careful.)

Finally, identify any gaps. If you realize there are key results that none of your current to-do list items will help achieve, you'll want to add ideas to your *Start Doing* list in service of those key results.

Prioritizing Your Work for the Next Quarter

With a filtered backlog of both pre-OKR work and new solution ideas, you are now ready to **prioritize the work you will do in the coming quarter.** We've described this process in Chapter 10. Your goal at this stage, though, isn't to create a detailed plan. Rather, you're laying out what you expect to work on in the next quarter or two, and you're doing it in a way that results in an ordered priority list of ideas to investigate.

Also in Chapter 10, we laid out a rubric for prioritizing your work based on each one's perceived level of risk versus its perceived level of value. Here's the diagram again:

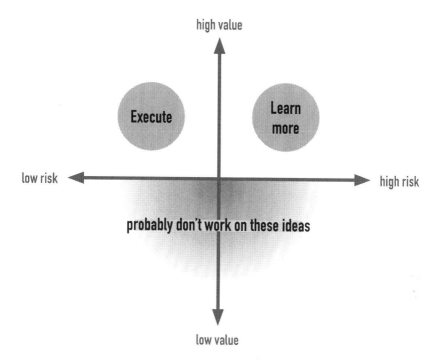

This prioritized list is your loose plan for the next quarter.

Build a Roadmap Driven by Key Results

Loose plans inevitably need to be codified to a degree. After all, we don't know a single leader that won't ask for some kind of formal future work plan to understand how you'll spend your time and achieve your goals. It's beneficial for you and your teams to understand the timeline of your work, too. These plans are often called **Roadmaps**.

Typically, roadmaps focus on outputs, dates, and budgets: *We'll do this work. It will be done by this date. It will cost this much.* This is the dominant way of planning, despite the fact that not a single person says, "I love Google Maps because it was shipped on time" or "I love my Apple Watch because it was produced on budget."

Of course, there is a time and place for output-based and date-driven planning: when uncertainty is low, when you know exactly what work needs to be done, when you have a solid understanding of how people will respond to the work, or there is low risk in doing the work.

But output-based planning doesn't make sense for the high-uncertainty work that OKRs encourage us to take on. When we're trying to solve complex problems, we're not done when we've made a thing. We're done when we achieve the result. We're planning in terms of achieving our goals, not simply getting through our to-do list.

This doesn't mean that we should throw out roadmaps altogether, however. It means redefining them and creating more responsive, outcome-based roadmaps instead. How do we do that?

Step 1: Change the question.

The first thing we need to do is change the question we're asking our teams with our roadmap.

The old questions: What will we build? When will we be done?

The new questions: **What results are we seeking? What outcomes are we trying to create? What will people be doing differently if we succeed?**

The answers to the old questions focus on output. The answers to the new questions focus on outcomes.

Step 2: Embrace learning activities.

In Chapter 9, we talked about the importance of learning and learning activities. Building learning activities into our working processes means including that work in our planning and then communicating our plans to do that work in our roadmaps.

This can be an uphill battle. We all think we know the answers—this is especially true for leaders at successful companies. People think their success shows that they know what customers want and that they and their teams will be able to continue to deliver successfully without question. As we've said time and again, there are many assumptions in that, which means a lot of unnecessary risk.

Learning activities can provide more answers—and better answers—than your guesses can. Acknowledging that and approaching your work from that perspective gives you the opportunity to try to understand your work more completely. As a result, you'll be able to solve real problems for real people, not potential problems you predict your potential customers might have...potentially.

Step 3: Build an outcome-based product roadmap.

When we think of roadmaps, we expect them to help us find our way to our destinations. Instead of thinking about a roadmap as a fixed plan that will get you there, think about your outcome-based roadmap as a communication tool that shows your intentions.

The destination of your roadmap is your OKR—getting people to change their behavior in the way you're targeting. With this newly defined destination, outcome-based roadmaps need to include a few key components to keep the focus on the right things as you move forward: strategic themes and organizational OKRs, your team's quarterly OKR goals, learning items, and solution ideas.

Here's a template we use for outcome-based product roadmaps:

Annual OKR			
Quarterly OKR	**Quarterly OKR**	**Quarterly OKR**	**Quarterly OKR**
Potential work items			
▪ ▬▬▬▬	• ▬▬▬▬	• ▬▬▬▬	• ▬▬▬▬
▪ ▬▬▬▬	• ▬▬▬▬		
▪ ▬▬▬▬			
▪ ▬▬▬▬			
▪ ▬▬▬▬			
Learning activities			
▪ ▬▬▬▬	• ▬▬▬▬		
▪ ▬▬▬▬	• ▬▬▬▬		

Strategic themes and organizational OKR:
These are the high-level, organizational objectives set by executive leaders that point teams in a specific direction for the year ahead. These might be things like "expand our market share in Europe" or "leverage the underutilized time our carrier fleet isn't ferrying passengers to deliver other goods and food." There can be multiple themes running in parallel for a larger organization, but different teams should be working on each one.

Quarterly KR goals:
These are the outcomes—the customer behavior changes—that your team will focus on in the upcoming quarter. These metrics tell you when you're "done." We're using quarters, again, because that's the most common period of time teams use with OKRs and it's less than a year (the typical planning cycle for most companies). If, however, quarters don't make sense for your team, adjust your timeframes as necessary.

Potential work items and solution ideas:
These is where the work items from your filtered list will appear, often as hypotheses. These are the things that you believe will allow you to achieve your goals. It's important to note here that what you're committing to are the key results, not the specific solution ideas you've listed; that's variable.

Learning activities:
In Chapter 9, we talked about the process of deciding whether a work item is an execution item, where you'll just start doing, building, or delivering something, or a learning activity, where you'll be answering important questions about the work. It's important to

*communicate learning work on your roadmap. You'll
want to represent important questions, unknowns, and
risks, here in this portion of the roadmap.*

This quarter, next quarter, the quarters beyond:
*Here's a basic truth: The farther out in time you look,
the less accurately you can predict what you're going
to work on. Looking just one quarter in advance, your
teams can make strong, well-educated guesses about
what solution ideas they think will achieve their goals.
Looking two quarters ahead, those guesses become less
confident. That means you should commit to fewer of
them. Three and four quarters out—six and nine months
from now—you really can't predict what you'll be working on, so there should be even fewer guesses on your
roadmaps for those periods.*

Of course, you may have some date-driven work and some other hard commitments (see *"date-driven work"* below). It's fine to place these items on a roadmap like this. Just make sure to clarify the difference between outcome-driven work and date-driven work.

And remember, your roadmaps are living documents. You will learn in the next quarter or two how well your first ideas worked, what moved the needle forward, and what your next guesses should be. You can then fill the boxes for Q3 and Q4 as you synthesize and act on your learnings from Q1 and Q2.

A good roadmap is a powerful communication tool. It creates transparency. It demonstrates humility. It embodies agility.

Step 4: Review your roadmaps at the beginning of each new cycle.

In many organizations, roadmap reviews happen once a year. With OKRs, this happens during your check-ins. Check-ins are where you present the data, review your results, and share what you learned. They're where you review your plans for the next period of work and discuss how or if those plans need to change. **Operating this way allows you to adjust course based on evidence in a continuous way.**

Think about it this way: If you've ever walked through a fog, you know you can't see 20 steps in front of you. You might be able to see only five steps. So, take the next five steps. Once you've taken the next five steps, the next five after that become clear. If the path is unobstructed—great, you can continue to go five steps further at a time—not 10, 15, or 20. In all likelihood, at some point, you're going to come across something that blocks your path, and you'll have to take a turn in one direction or even go back a few steps. But you're going to make evidence-based decisions just in time, instead of blindly running through the fog and smacking into a tree, stepping off a cliff, or hitting an iceberg. You're discovering what you need to do as you move forward and making decisions accordingly.

The same is true of your roadmaps—which means that as you learn new things, your roadmaps will shift. It's possible that your OKRs will stay the same (it's also possible they will change), but the products (the things you're making) are variable. The commitments you make are to the behavior changes. The products and solutions you pursue will change depending on what kinds of behavior change you are or are not able to achieve along the way. Sometimes you'll build something, scale it, and double down on it. Sometimes you're going to try something, realize it's not going to work, and kill it so you can try something new.

How to Handle Date-Driven Work

Work with OKRs is generally progress-driven, not date-driven. In other words, instead of deadlines and milestones, we use results as the measure of progress. However, in order to achieve progress, sometimes we do need to set some dates and get certain things done by specific deadlines. That's normal.

Say your company makes vitamins and you're looking to attract a younger subset of customers. So, you decide to hire young comics to create video ads for social media. Naturally, you'll need to hire those comics by a certain date, approve the scripts by another date, and film and edit the videos by another. Traditional, date-driven product management works fine for this.

Here's the thing though: Whenever you can, you are going to want to make two small but important changes when you're planning date-driven work.

First, you're going to want to **reduce the scope of the date-driven work**. So, instead of hiring 30 young comics right off the bat and filming a full library of videos—and taking months to do so—start with just two comics. Film just two short videos, and get that done within two weeks. See how those perform on social media and go from there.

Second, **make sure that each small batch of work will be able to generate a result**. So, instead of breaking up the project by stage—for example, first we write the script, then we create the storyboards, then we make the video—instead, we try to get to a small, short, valuable video as quickly as we can.

Our goal with both of these tactics is to be able to test the work quickly and to see if it's worth continuing down this path. By keeping the scope of the work small and insisting on creating even a tiny amount of customer-centric value, we can remove a lot of the risk and uncertainty from date-driven work.

Work That Has Seasonality

Think of accountants. In the United States, the deadline to file taxes is April 15, which means accounting firms need to help their clients hit that very real deadline every year. Think of retailers, too, many of whom have seasonal businesses—perhaps they make a huge percentage of their annual sales during the Christmas season. They need to complete certain tasks in time for holiday shopping season or they risk missing the mark on their key results and broader objectives in a big way. Having these big deadlines doesn't mean you can't use OKRs. It means you reframe how you work toward those deadlines.

In these kinds of deadlines, there are usually two kinds of work. There's the routine and well-understood work. (Accountants need to file certain forms by certain dates.) There's also work that is predictable but has some risk in it. Accountants need to collect receipts, paperwork, and documents from their clients. What's the best way to do this? People are notoriously avoidant about their taxes.

OKRs are great for the second kind of work. An accounting firm might set a key result around getting their customers to submit all of their paperwork on time, for example. OKRs are less useful for the routine, the predictable, and the well-understood.

When You Need to Hit a Deadline

There are times when you face hard, external deadlines. Years ago when we were operating our product development studio, Neo, we did a project for a nonprofit organization that wanted to build a new and ambitious web-based service. And they had a deadline: It needed to be done in time for their annual conference—in nine months.

This deadline was important. The conference was an opportunity to show their grantors the progress of the initiatives those grantors had funded the previous year. That year, the grantors had given their organization a lot of money to build this new service.

The service in question would be a web-based portal, designed to connect volunteers with organizations needing volunteers. The portal our client imagined came with a long and ambitious list of requirements. It was our job to build this portal. In nine months.

We really wanted to help them. It was a great project, a great mission. It was also, given the deadline and the enormous scope of work, pretty close to impossible.

This is a problem that we're sure you recognize. You've got an important target with an important deadline and an impossibly large scope. So how do you handle it? One way is to focus on the OKR.

The client's objective was to **create the best way for volunteers to match with and begin working with organizations that needed volunteers** and to do that within nine months—in time for their conference. When we sat down with them to define the key results, our conversation revolved around setting initial targets. *What will we need to achieve by the date of the conference that will demonstrate to your grantors that we've made meaningful progress and that we were spending the grant money well?* We came up with the following:

- 100 volunteers in the system
- 10 organizations seeking volunteers in the system
- 10 matches made between volunteers and organizations
- 1 volunteer project underway or completed

Then, we asked the hard question. "What if we delivered those key results by the conference and had an operational website but without *any* of the features on your wish list?" As a team, we made the hard decision. We would walk away from "requirements" and instead focus on results. The client told us that as long as they had the results and a website to show their grantors in October, they'd be happy.

So, that's what we did. We put all our energy into executing and learning work that focused on the critical questions we faced. *Could we get organizations to sign up in the system? Could we get volunteers? Did we provide value to them once they were there?* And so on. Instead of spending months building specific features that may or may not have effectively delivered the key results we needed, we spent months ensuring we were building something that did. You can still operate with dates and deadlines, but your OKRs serve as the filter through which you meet those deadlines.

Key Takeaways

1. Planning work is a part of every organization, but it doesn't look the same with OKRs as it traditionally does because you don't plan specific output, and the plans you do create aren't fixed. Your plans can change as you learn things from the market—and that's the point. You want to enthusiastically embrace uncertainty and course correction.

2. If you have planned work when you transition to OKRs, filter that list of projects and ideas through your new OKRs to determine what from that list still fits—what will help you achieve your key results. The projects that fit stay on the priority list.

3. The world today changes quickly, and customers change quickly with it. Linear, output-based planning models don't account for the need to respond to that change. With OKRs, you use responsive, outcome-based roadmaps instead. The further out in time you get from the present, the less you can predict the specifics of your work because you don't know what your customers will need or want at that time.

4. If we previously asked, "What will we build?" change the question to "What will people be doing differently if we succeed?" *Those outcomes* are what you target in your planning.

Part 4

Making OKRs Successful in Your Organization

We've said that OKRs are three things: a *goal-setting framework*, which we described in Part 2; a *process*, which we described in Part 3; and **a culture. This part of the book is all about OKR culture.**

This section takes a look at what leaders—from executives to middle managers to team leads—need to do in order to make OKRs a success. (We'll give you one hint right now: You can't just set it and forget it.) We'll discuss the key elements of OKR culture and how can create that culture.

We'll ask you to think for a moment about *why* you want to use OKRs in your organization. OKRs can solve many problems—and the way you use them will change based on the problem that you want to solve. Thinking about *why* is a critical step.

We'll also take a look at OKRs at scale. What if you have 500 teams in your company? Can OKRs work in that reality? The answer is yes, and this section will cover exactly how.

Let's go.

Chapter 13

Start with Why

Simon Sinek's TED talk "How great leaders inspire action" has been watched over 11 million times.[14] We'll be honest with you—it's really annoying. Simon repeats the phrase, "People don't buy what you do, they buy *why* you do it," so many times. It drives us crazy. Here's the even more annoying part: He's absolutely right.

Anytime you want someone to buy something—a product, an idea, or a way of working—you need to explain to them, first, *why* this is something they should care about. As we've been working on this book, we've realized that this was a huge missing part of most OKR conversations. Most of the time, leaders bring in OKRs to an organization and then people in the organization immediately start trying to use them. The problem here is that people generally have *no idea why* they need to adopt this aside from "The boss said so." People respond begrudgingly, if at all. Soon, using OKRs becomes a chore, people resent it, and it fails. We saw this with Agile as well.

To make OKRs succeed you have to start with *why*. (Thank you, Simon.)

---

14   https://youtu.be/u4ZoJKF_VuA?si=H7axOwcYR_qBSXHW

What's the Problem We're Solving?

If you're a leader introducing a new way of working (especially a new way to set goals) to your organization, you need to explain to your staff *before* you start implementing the new system what problem this addresses. We guarantee that your company had a goal-setting framework before it tried OKRs. What was wrong with it? How was it no longer meeting the needs of the business? What proof do we have of that? What are we trying to achieve that the current system can't help us with? This is the first conversation leaders need to have with their organization when it's time to implement OKRs.

> *For years we've measured success in terms of hitting our production targets. We've made many great products (and some not-so-great ones). The reality is that most of our customers don't use most of our products. Worse, it takes us a long time to figure out whether or not our customers are using our products. Worst of all, we frequently have no idea why. We've failed to get close to our customers.*
>
> *This has forced us to support and maintain these products, costing us millions each year with no obvious ROI or customer benefit.*
>
> *These products were the result of the agendas of various leaders and failed to align us around a cohesive strategy. We missed multiple collaboration opportunities and wasted too much on duplicate efforts across the company that were unaware of one another. This needs to change. We're switching to OKRs to avoid this happening in the future.*

Boom! You've framed the problem space for your staff. You know what else you did? You showed some humility and admitted some mistakes in the past (this goes a long way).

Here's what's next...

What Will the Future Look Like?

Now that you've defined the reason for the change—the "why" (thanks, again, Simon)—you need to paint a picture of what success will look like in the future. Instead of continuing down the path that got you to where you are today, you're going to change things up so that the organization behaves differently in the future. Share that vision with your teams.

> *Our goal is to become a customer-centric organization that deeply understands the people that we serve and can meet their needs with valuable offerings.*
>
> *We want to become a learning organization that can respond quickly to changes in the marketplace. We want to be able to sense when we've chosen a poor direction and we want to be able to admit it, then quickly pivot to a better alternative.*
>
> *We want to empower everyone to learn whether their work is having a positive impact on our customers and to feel safe to speak up and change things when they learn that it isn't.*
>
> *Finally, we want to create a culture that celebrates the success of our customers rather than just the delivery of products to market. OKRs will help us achieve this.*

Wow! Now we've got a destination.

The last step...

What Will Get Us from Here to There?

The last part of the framing leaders need to put in place prior to implementing OKRs (or any other major change to the organization's way of working) is their hypothesis for how we're going to get from the current condition to the future state. The change must be framed as a hypothesis, one that has clear success criteria, expressed as outcomes. What will *we* be doing differently once we've embraced this change? In this way, you're not mandating a change blindly. You're offering a proposed solution where the measure of success isn't the deployment of the solution (that's an output) but rather the visible changes in culture and behavior you laid out in your future state vision.

> *We want to change our goal-setting framework, moving away from rewarding output and delivery and toward measuring success in terms of outcomes. We are going to implement OKRs to help us set new goals and work in this new way.*
>
> *We believe that OKRs provide the right framework to get us all thinking about the customer first. We'll know it's working when we see the customer's needs considered in the majority of our strategic decisions, a reduction in the time it takes us to learn if we've chosen the right work to do, and significant increases in the most important and most valuable behaviors of our customers.*

Ta-da! You've laid out the hypothesis for the new goal-setting framework in a way that ties together the problem statement and the future state. In addition, you've put in success criteria that will help both you and your teams determine if the OKR implementation has been successful. Ticking the box is no longer enough to say it worked.

Start with Why

If we want any change to work, we need to let folks know why we're changing. Forcing the change is always an option, but it will inevitably lead to resentment, frustration, and confusion. Putting forward a problem statement, a vision for a positive future state, and a hypothesis for the proposed process/culture/method change lays a foundation your teams can rally behind. It also gives you the flexibility to adjust your course as you move forward. After all, you will inevitably learn things along the way. You want to be able to take advantage of that learning. Having a flexible hypothesis and a clear statement of why will make these adjustments easier. It's in your best interest to start with why.

Key Takeaways

1. **Start with why.**
   OKRs are a tool to help you improve your organization, but they're not a cure-all. Why do you want to use OKRs? What are you trying to improve? What problem are you solving? Be clear about that before you start.

2. **Get people invested.**
   People are motivated by *the why*. Your job, once you've clarified the reason for the change is communicate it. And then communicate it some more. Be clear about the vision to build buy-in. What will be better on the other side? How will people's lives improve? How will our shared future improve?

Chapter 14

Supporting OKRs from the Top

Recently, we spoke to a former CEO who had been hired to turn around an ailing tech company. The company had been in a multi-year slump, and the CEO had ideas about how to change that. One of his first orders of business was to implement OKRs.

He wanted to use OKRs to create a more customer-focused organization. He hoped that, through the process, teams would gain the trust, autonomy, and psychological safety to discover and deploy products that would be customer-centric and would raise the company out of its slump.

His instinct was to go big—to change the entire organization all at once. He launched an ambitious initiative: training the entire organization on OKRs. Immediately though, the problems began, showing up in the form of two huge roadblocks.

First, the sales organization revolted. They didn't understand why they had to implement OKRs. They already had goals, set for each salesperson. Building a "team based" approach to achieving goals was unappealing, especially for high-performing salespeople who didn't want to "carry" their less successful colleagues on their back.

Second, the product development teams had no idea what to do once their OKRs were set. Once the OKRs were written, they realized that the OKRs didn't tell them what features to build. This was an entirely new situation for them. They had no idea how to make the process successful.

They weren't used to answering the question, "What should we build?" This is the central question of the OKR process, but the organization had never developed those skills. They were paralyzed.

Change is hard.

We want to say that again: Change is hard. Good change. Well-intentioned change. Bad change. All change is hard. OKRs promise tremendous benefits to organizations that adopt them, but to gain those benefits, things need to change—and those benefits need to be made clear to everyone.

The most important predictor of success when going through any change is consistent and continuous leadership support.

For OKRs specifically, we've certainly seen organizations that have had limited local success at the team, workgroup, or department level. That kind of change can certainly begin with grass-roots initiatives, but even this kind of change needs local leadership support to sustain itself.

For widespread OKR success, you need the people who lead the organization to be active and continuous champions of OKRs. They are the ones who must create the time, resources, incentives, training, support structures, and culture that allow OKR success. They must explain the benefits of OKRs and ensure everyone has the skills to succeed in the new reality. And this support cannot be a one-shot effort. Leaders must expect to be champions of this way of working for as long as they want to use OKRs. Implementing OKRs is not a superficial change.

So, leaders, we're talking to you in this chapter. Your support will dictate not only how successful your teams will be using OKRs, but also the likelihood and speed at which they will achieve their—and your—goals. To see that happen, you need to support your teams' OKR efforts in the following ways:

1. Start with why.
2. Provide a clear strategy and high-level OKRs first.
3. Trust the process and your teams.
4. Support learning work.

5. Provide universal access to data.
6. Create a safe culture of learning.
7. Model the values you want to see in your culture.
8. Design the organization for collaboration and agility.

Start with Why

Change for change's sake is theater. It's a transparent gimmick leaders use to "shake things up" when they're unhappy with something. It's obvious and often resented by most employees. We wrote a bit more about this in Chapter 13, so we'll keep it brief here. If you're going to rewrite goals for the entire company, you must first explain to your staff why you're doing it. Lay out the benefits each of them will gain from the new system. Explain how it will benefit your customers. Reassure everyone that they will be trained to succeed in the new world.

Provide a Clear Strategy and High-Level OKRs First

We've worked with too many organizations who look to OKRs as a cure-all. *When we implement our OKRs, everything will be better.* Then, when teams sit down in their workshops to write OKRs, they look across the room at one another and ask, "What's the most important thing for us to do next year?" Or, "We have too many things to work on! Everything is Priority 1! What do our leaders think is most important?"

Let's go back to the beginning—the reasons that we're using OKRs in the first place. Of the many benefits that we discussed in Part 1 of this book, two of the most important are **focus** and **alignment**.

Both of these are dependent on strategy. Without strategy, how will people know what to focus on? Without strategy, what will people align around?

Unless you provide clear answers to these questions in the form of a clear strategy and high-level OKRs, your organization will struggle to benefit from OKRs.

For more about strategy, see Chapter 4.

Trust the Process and Your Teams

OKRs replace command and control leadership with **aligned autonomy**. Leaders use strategy and OKRs to create alignment, and then ask the teams to work with a great deal of autonomy within those constraints.

This is one of the hardest changes leaders need to make when adopting OKRs: changing the way they lead teams. For decades, the business world has trained leaders at all levels (executives, department heads, team managers, etc.) to tell people what to do. The overwhelming majority of leaders we've worked with believe that's their primary responsibility. Most often, this manifests as leaders prescribing specific things for teams to do or make and providing explicit deadlines by which to do or make them. This is what we mean by *command and control*.

This approach certainly has its appeal: You always know (or think you know) what your teams are working on. And your teams can usually provide you with a clear statement of what they're doing whenever you come by to check on them. Though this approach promises to offer leaders peace of mind, it also implies that these leaders don't trust their teams to make decisions on their own. It assumes that the "boss knows best" and that the leader's ideas will assuredly meet customer needs and solve business problems, even if there's no guarantee of that.

OKRs remove prescription from the equation. If you're writing your OKRs correctly, you're not including explicit solutions as part of your goals. You're writing the outcomes you want to see. From there, it's up to your teams to figure out what activities will best achieve those outcomes. The teams are, after all, closest to the work. They're the subject matter experts that you hired for their expertise, so why not let them use it?

Of course, the ideas the teams come up with need to align with the organization's high-level OKRs, fall within a reasonable scope of work, and remain on brand, all of which leaders can and should advise on. But for OKRs to work, the teams doing the work *must* be the ones brainstorming and creating their work plans. Leaders need to step back and let that happen. You need to trust your teams. Not only will it breed greater trust between you and your employees on the whole, but it will also help teams become and stay passionate about their work. When they get to implement their own ideas, their energy and excitement grows.

That doesn't mean, though, that they get to drive away with the keys, never to return.

Note: Trusting your teams isn't always enough. Ensuring your teams know how to proceed once the prescriptive assignments have been removed is also essential. Let's be honest, it's a lot easier to just "do what the boss says." You must also train your teams in learning methods and continuously reinforce through rewards, celebration, and incentive that changing their idea midstream based on evidence they collect along the way is not only OK but the desired goal.

Trust Requires Transparent Communication—from All Sides

Aligned autonomy requires **transparency.**

If leaders don't know exactly what their teams are working on, anxiety can set in, bringing with it the desire to micromanage. Instead of micromanaging, put the onus on the team to keep you in the loop. Make it clear that you're trusting them to make these decisions but that you also need radical transparency from them in the process. Your teams should communicate (or even over-communicate) regularly and frequently to you about:

- What they're working on
- The progress they're making toward their OKRs
- What they're learning
- What they plan on changing based on what they've learned

This communication doesn't need to be a heavy responsibility. It could be as simple as a weekly email with the four bullet points above and their corresponding responses. But it is important that it happens. It allows you, as leaders, to have a clear understanding of what your teams are doing at all times, along with the rationale behind their decisions. Plus, it quashes the urge to prescribe and micromanage. And if you do find something worth discussing with the team, you can get involved before the idea or experiment gets too far downstream.

The way you respond to these updates is important, too. Respond in ways that encourage more sharing. Ask questions but try to avoid overruling their decisions. (See below: *Create a safe culture of learning*.)

Making OKRs work as a leader is a two-way street, but it starts with trust. It takes time to find the right level of communication, one that ensures you get the information you need from your teams while giving them the freedom they need to do their best work.

Support Learning Work

If you as a leader are not telling teams what to do, then what does it look like for your teams to operate without prescribed task lists? The task lists, work plans, and product roadmaps that guided your teams before may hold some promising ideas, but how can you and your teams *be certain* which set of activities will deliver your target key results? The short answer is you can't. Unless you experiment and look at the data and feedback you get from customers—again and again and again. That's learning work. And that's a critical piece of the **agility** that OKRs can bring to organizations, if leaders can allow that to happen.

As we talked about in Chapter 10, teams use learning-centric ways of working to learn more about their customers and to understand the problems they're having. They take a learning and experimental mindset to figuring out the best ways to solve their customers' problems. Leaders choosing to implement OKRs in their organizations must also train their teams in these kinds of approaches to their work and give them the support (time and resources) to be able to do it not just once, but continuously.

Why is it so crucial?

Balance Evidence and Educated Guesses

A big part of this work is analyzing the evidence and data you collect from your customers' interactions with your work then determining your next moves based on what you learn from that information. If you don't look at that data, how are you making decisions about what to work on? You're likely guessing.

When teams make project plans and task lists based on hunches or assumptions instead of evidence, they're doing the same thing: guessing.

It's fine to guess. In fact, we'd venture to guess (see what we did there?) that every important scientific breakthrough started with a hunch or a guess. But after that guess came the hard work of scientific discovery: gathering evidence to see if the guesses were right.

Work is the same way. Of course, we can make guesses about what we should be working on. But how long should we work on something, and how much money should we spend on it, before we go and get the evidence?

In a discovery-centric way of working, we see our work as a set of hypotheses to be tested. We embrace research as the way to test our ideas. We set ambitious goals but lean into humility. We know where we want to go, but we admit that we're not certain how to get there.

Unfortunately, that's a hard change for many organizations to embrace. We recently heard how difficult this can be from a client of ours. We'd worked hard to help them kick off their OKR journey within a part of the organization, and together we created a set of OKRs to get them moving. So imagine how we felt when we got this email:

> *"Though in theory we should allow experimentation and discovery, this hasn't happened. Instead, business stake-holders gave us a strategy that said, 'We need to start selling in the United States.' For our teams, this means we have to do everything to build and launch our services in the United States, and there's no room for any other activity in the next 12-month period. We ended up going into waterfall delivery mode. Leadership implied that the*

'strategy' is an order for a piece of work to be delivered within the shortest time frame."

In this story, the "strategy" from leaders wasn't really a strategy. It was a command and control style order. When the old command and control instincts come out, OKRs become just another way to deliver orders. This is ironic, because if that old way of working had been creating results, leadership would never have tried OKRs in the first place.

What's particularly disappointing about prescriptive command and control ways of working is that they squander many opportunities for course correction, agility, and customer-centricity. In fact, the customer has been erased from the conversation completely. Organizations that treat OKRs as just a rebranding of the previous ways of working get very little benefit from them, and in fact, often abandon them (as did the client above).

Building Empathy for the Customer

Research requires teams to be in frequent communication with customers—both end consumers and internal customers. This means your teams are getting firsthand knowledge of the problems experienced by the people they serve. They hear stories and feedback that help them put themselves in their customers' shoes.

When done well, the active, inbound stream of insight that's provided through research can also help you quickly spot themes in customer behaviors and make sense of the data that your analytics tools are capturing. Research allows your people to combine learning from direct feedback with what they see in the analytics, gaining a greater understanding of customer needs. This understanding can be the basis for better solutions to customer problems. It can be the basis for better team collaboration and productivity, too. It can also mean better efficiency and efficacy from third-party vendors. In other words, if we offer better solutions for whoever our teams serve, we'll get better results for the organization.

Provide Universal Access to Data

Data—both qualitative and quantitative—is the heart of successful OKR implementation. Teams across the company need access to it, unfettered by technology and corporate politics. The easier it is for teams to access the data, the faster they can make decisions and move forward. Make access to data the path of least resistance. Invest in analytics and reporting tools everyone can learn to use. Ensure that every system deployed in the company—be it an expense tracking program or a learning management system—comes with a reporting tool. Provide access to industry reports and analyses. Your teams will thank you.

What does this look like for non-tech teams? If you're a lawyer or you work in HR, for instance, you probably don't have all the quantitative usage data about your products and services at your fingertips. If you're serving internal customers—other employees of the company—you're probably not even sure what "usage data" *is* for the things you produce. And you certainly may not have a system that captures this data automatically.

Think about what you expect others to do with the work you produce. What behavior does it enable? For example, if you work in talent acquisition, you might measure the amount of time it takes you to fill a position and the turnover rate of that position. If you work in the legal department implementing vendor onboarding and procurement policies, you may want to see how long, on average, it takes a vendor to get through that process and how much support they need along the way.

Regardless of the behavior you're trying to improve, you will need to start tracking this data—or figure out how to track this data—and ensure that every team member who works on an aspect of this work knows how, when, and where to input their pieces of data from there forward.

In all of these cases, if you can cut out any middlemen (middle teams?) that sit between your teams and the data they need, do it. The faster teams can understand how their work is affecting customers, the sooner they can react to it.

Create a Safe Culture of Learning

For many organizations, the changes we've just described—setting strategy then trusting teams to pursue it and setting objectives then allowing teams to discover their way forward—are huge shifts in organizational culture. These shifts focus on learning, which is key for OKR success. Though we could write a book about building a culture of learning (wait... we did, it's called *Sense & Respond* and, as a leader, you should absolutely read it), we want to focus here on two specific things leaders can do to build these kinds of cultures: **Foster psychological safety** and **celebrate learning in everything**.

Foster Psychological Safety

Working with a client's team last year, we were encouraging them to build a regular, weekly cadence of customer interviews to inform the ongoing development of their new B2C communications tool. The tool had gotten a large number of downloads immediately after its first release, and our client received more than enough feedback, requests, complaints, and reviews to give them a mountain of things to work on. The team was enthusiastic, but they faced a problem: "With all this information, how do we prioritize what to work on first?" they asked.

We were also enthusiastic. Together with the team, we decided that the best way to answer that question was with customer research. After all, there's no better way to make customer-centric decisions than by digging into firsthand customer research. We helped the client write an interview guide, identify customers to speak to, and helped them make a plan to complete their first round of interviews in the coming week.

And then...crickets.

A week went by. No interviews.

Two weeks later, still nothing.

We reached out to the team lead to see what was going on. He told us that they didn't want to bring their research plan to leadership. They were worried that the higher-ups would think that they were questioning leadership's directives. It was hard to speak up at the company. People had seen former colleagues get chewed out for questioning leadership.

People had been fired for making mistakes. So the team was reluctant to bring up their ideas and questions with leadership.

Sadly, this is a familiar story.

It made us realize that though we can teach objectives and key results, train teams to focus on outcomes, and tout the benefits of learning work, all of that will fail without psychological safety.

The term "psychological safety" was coined by Harvard Business School professor Amy Edmondson, who defines it as "a belief that one will not be punished or humiliated for speaking up with ideas, questions, concerns, or mistakes, and that the team is safe for interpersonal risk-taking." It's the ability to speak with candor, regardless of how benign or controversial your thoughts may be, without worrying whether you'll still be employed at the end of the day.

This team we were working with knew their product had tremendous potential. They knew they had to discover how to prioritize bug fixes, enhancements, and new features to deliver an ever-better customer experience. But they lacked the psychological safety to actually go and do the research. To their leaders, the mere act of talking to customers implied that the leaders' direction might not be correct, and the team felt that their leaders couldn't tolerate that.

Even worse, if the team did do research and their findings contradicted their leaders' directives, there was no safe forum in which the team could share their insights. This made the whole research process pointless. When there's no safety, you can't benefit from research. No research means no learning. And without learning, there's no way to find the best solutions or to change direction when you need to.

An underlying premise of OKRs is that there is never only one way to solve a problem. Instead of operating as if the first answer is the right answer, teams should be prepared to try several hypotheses; inevitably, some of their hypotheses will be wrong.

Working this way means that teams will need to feel comfortable going to their leaders and saying, "Hey boss, we got this wrong. We thought it was going to work, but it didn't. Here's what we learned, and here's what we're planning on doing next." If teams fear getting reprimanded, belittled, or fired for being wrong, this doesn't work. Innovation and creativity get stifled. People stop asking questions and instead choose the safe option, shying away from taking risks. They will do whatever is least likely to get them yelled at—whether or not it's the best option on the table.

The message teams receive when leaders behave this way is not just that they can't ever be wrong, but also that leadership doesn't value learning and isn't invested in their teams' capacity, potential, and growth.

Leaders, if you want your organizations to be truly innovative and agile (that's lowercase "a" agile for you product and software folks), you need to send the message that your teams' insights are important—that what they learn is equally as valuable as what they build (and sometimes more so). An easy way to start doing this is to change the questions you ask your teams. Instead of "What are you working on?" or "When will the new campaign launch?" ask: "What did you learn this week?" Impress upon your teams that you want them to learn continuously and to use that learning in their day-to-day work.

Celebrate Learning in Everything

In his 2016 TED talk "The Unexpected Benefit of Celebrating Failure,"[15] Astro Teller, the head of Google's X moonshot factory (not to be confused with the social media platform formerly known as Twitter), talks about how he builds a culture that celebrates learning by making learning *the path of least resistance*. The teams he works with build learning into every development cycle. And when they learn something that contradicts their hypothesis, even if it forces them to abandon an entire initiative, he gives them "hugs and high fives." Why?

Teller wants to make sure his teams are always spending their time on the ideas most likely to succeed. As soon as they realize they're headed down a wrong path, they correct their course, and these pivots are held up as winning examples of good work. Instead of burying them under the rug, teams share them across the whole company letting everyone

---

15   Teller, Astro, "The Unexpected Benefit of Celebrating Failure." 2016
    https://www.ted.com/talks/astro_teller_the_unexpected_benefit_of_
    celebrating_failure

learn from their efforts. So, as much as they get excited about launching a successful idea, they're just as excited about killing an idea that isn't going to work. It's not expenditure; it's progress and cost savings.

If we build a psychologically safe culture of learning, our teams believe that learning is a part of their work and valued as much as delivery work. They explore their options eagerly, knowing that pivoting away from them is viewed as progress. OKRs demand this type of culture to succeed. It comes back to our principles—specifically, autonomy, customer-centricity, and most of all, agility. OKRs can give your organizations all of those things if you, as leaders, ensure your teams feel safe and even celebrated when they experiment, learn, and pivot.

Model the Values You Want to See in Your Culture

We said early on in this book that OKRs are a tool, a way of working, and a culture. For new cultures to take hold, leaders must model them. This is, in our minds, the most powerful thing leaders can do. It's one thing to talk about new values—or even put a ton of resources behind new processes and systems to support them. It's quite another thing to walk the walk, to show your teams that you're right there in the trenches with them.

Leaders have a tendency to want to appear in control. After all, we want our people to be confident, so we want to behave in ways that create confidence. But when we're moving away from command and control and toward aligned autonomy, then we are actually giving up a degree of control. This is hard.

In a learning organization, you as a leader must demonstrate how much you value learning facts and data, even when those facts and data contradict what you may have said publicly. If you behave with rigidity and prescriptiveness or if you fail to acknowledge the facts and the data and the learning that your teams are creating, then your teams will inevitably give up on those ways of working.

If you're just starting to transform your organization's culture around learning—or if you haven't engaged with the process as a leader—you need to take the risk and model those behaviors yourself. Show your colleagues that nothing "bad" happens to anyone who learns and adjusts their direction—leaders included. Prove to your teams that you're listening to their insights. Use the evidence they have collected in your own decision-making.

And, truthfully, this behavior is so easy to model, you have no reason not to. We did some agile coaching work with teams at a major U.S. financial institution, including its president and entire C-suite. We were helping the whole organization adopt more agile ways of working, and the president had been a vocal champion of the change. Even with his leadership, though, people in the organization were struggling to make changes.

About six weeks into our engagement, the president held a big meeting with all of the VP-level team members who reported to him (about 150 people). Reporting on his own experience of trying to learn and use agile leadership methods, he made a very simple statement: "Agile is hard."

Everyone went bananas. We got so many emails from those VPs who couldn't believe what they'd heard. *How did you get him to understand this? He really gets it. Thank goodness, he knows what we're talking about!* He had said three words—just three words, and it entirely changed the tone of the team and their perception of his support for their work.

Why were these three words so powerful? Because they showed learning and, more importantly, humility. They demonstrated to people that leadership understood that they'd been asking for something that was difficult. They showed that it was OK to admit that something was harder than expected. Ultimately, they showed growth. This is what we mean when we say, "Model the behavior you want to see in your teams."

Leaders, your words and actions are more visible than anyone else's. What you say and do goes a long way. By modeling the behavior you want to see in your culture, you make room for change. The more teams and other leaders see your support for learning and experimentation, the likelier it is that real change will occur and that your organization's values will evolve.

Design the Organization for Collaboration and Agility

Think about it: Almost all organizations seek alignment in some way. One way we do that is by dividing people into teams according to function and expertise. In software systems, designers start off the project. Then, the engineers do their thing. They then hand it off to the operations team who deploys the software. In manufacturing, we get even more specific: The tire team starts, the wheel team takes over, then the chassis team finishes the job. (Those of you in car manufacturing, we give you license to rewrite the last sentence for greater accuracy.) These configurations may sound well-aligned from an internal production standpoint, but none of the teams in either of these contexts touch the end customer directly. Unless they're talking to other teams in the organization who do, how can the organization be sure they're best serving the customer be it an internal or external one? The short answer is, they can't.

Enable Reorganization

Early on in the book, we warned against writing your OKRs to fit the tasks on your existing to-do lists. In certain cases, you may find that some of those tasks are likely to help you achieve your OKRs and you should still do them. **But in many cases, you'll find that, with new goals, you've got plenty of new activities to work on. It's possible that some of those new activities may also require a new team or business entity altogether.** You may need to reorganize. That's another piece of the collaboration puzzle for organizations to anticipate.

A few years ago, we were conducting a workshop with several teams from a Midwestern industrial manufacturing company. One team described a problem they'd been trying to solve. One of the company's products was a pipe-bending machine designed for big construction projects—we're talking industrial-grade, heavy-metal pipes—which they sold for $750,000 apiece. The target buyers were general contractors. The problem, though, was that no one was buying the machines. It wasn't just a cost issue (how many pipes do you need to bend to justify an investment of three-quarters of a million dollars?); the machines were also heavy and cumbersome to transport, and contractors didn't want to drag them around to every construction site. But the company needed to figure out a way to make this machine work in their product lineup.

In coming up with alternatives, the team in charge of the success of the pipe-bending machine suggested "pipe-bending as a service." Instead of selling the machine outright, they'd sell the *value* of the machine. There were numerous routes they could take: They could rent the machine to customers for a given amount of time. They could transport the machine to construction sites and charge by the hour. They could even offer to do the pipe-bending for customers and charge by the pipe. No matter which way they went, though, they knew they were proposing a significant change: They'd be selling a service, not a direct product, which was a completely different offering for the company. That meant they couldn't just have a sales team in charge of the product's success. They needed a cross-functional team of pipe-benders, general contractors, salespeople, and engineers to collaborate and figure out the best way to deliver the new pipe-bending service.

The solution idea had a great possibility of leading to beneficial changes in customer behavior: The customers were more likely to purchase the use of the pipe-bending machine at a lower price tag and lower inconvenience level than buying the machines outright. In turn, it could solve the company's problem of not making money on such an expensive product and thereby help meet a larger objective of earning more revenue and reducing sunk costs.

One big thing to remember here is that nobody would have come to this solution had they not collaborated across roles and departments (or at least it likely would have taken a whole lot longer to get there). The product team might have thought, "Well, we could put the machine on four wheels instead of two, or we could try to make it lighter. Those would make it easier to transport." The sales team could have considered lowering the price of the machine thinking that would bring more customers through the door. In the first example, they were looking at the problem through a product-specific lens. In the second, it was a sales-only lens. In the end, the solution they needed came from looking at the problem from several different points of view.

The other big thing to remember is that deciding to pursue the "pipe-bending as a service" route would mean the company needed to embrace making changes to internal teams and structures to see the service through. You may find yourself or your teams in similar situations. **When you look at the business through the lens of the OKRs you're working toward, your work is no longer local to one team: It's collective.** It's less important to keep things the way they are for the sake of convention than it is to solve your customers' problems and achieve your goals. That means being open to change and embracing the collaboration that comes from it.

How Collaboration Enables Alignment and Customer-centricity

We were speaking to our friend Sophie earlier this year after she'd had one of these experiences with her health insurance company. Sophie has medical, dental, and vision insurance all through the same large U.S. health insurance company. Though she'd had no issue with receiving medical benefits over the course of the year, when she tried to make a dental appointment, her insurance appeared inactive to the dentist's office even though it appeared "active" on her account's portal through the insurance company.

So, she called the number on her insurance card. The representative told her she'd reached the medical insurance division; she needed to call the dental division. When she called that number, three different representatives passed her off before someone could help resolve the issue. Finally, with her dental coverage sorted, Sophie figured she should make sure her vision insurance wasn't also mistakenly inactive. Hoping it could be an easy check in the backend system (you'd think...), Sophie asked the last representative she was talking to if they could take a look. Perhaps not surprisingly, that rep couldn't even access her vision information. For that, she needed to call the vision division and speak to someone else. Another call! Another representative! Tired of waiting on hold and frustrated by having to call so many different numbers, Sophie gave up and hoped she'd be able to make an eye appointment when she needed one. Fingers crossed for Sophie.

The point of this story is not to call out insurance companies for bad customer service, but to show how clearly this insurance company does not put the customer experience first. There's no crossover between medical, dental, and vision departments even in the corporation's customer service operations, which means that customers who call with questions are often sent packing with a list of next steps *they* need to take, a list of problems *they* need to keep trying to solve for themselves. The customer has a frustrating experience, like Sophie did, and comes away with a worse impression of their insurance company than they had before. Customers like Sophie don't care about your company's org chart. To them, you are one company, one insurance provider (in this case). Considering the customer's perspective provides a clearer sense of how to reorganize especially in light of experiences like Sophie's, which are hardly unique.

We understand organizations like insurance companies need to work around a lot of red tape and legal constraints. But that doesn't mean they have to build their organizations *around* those constraints. In order to be customer-centric, organizations need to have an understanding of who their customers are and what they're looking for—and then build the organization *around the customer.*

CASE STUDY

Organizing for agility in an online classifieds marketplace

Organizational design plays an important role in the success of OKR deployment. In some cases, you may need to redesign your team structure to support a customer-centric OKR process.

That was the case for Hugo Froes and Timo Bolse, who led teams at OLX, an online classifieds marketplace. OLX operates in numerous marketplaces and many countries, which increases the complexity of any process change, including implementing OKRs. To combat this, Froes and Bolse reorganized their staff with the explicit goal of minimizing dependencies among them and ensuring that each new team structure, which they called tribes, focused on a specific customer.

In their new tribe-centric structure, each tribe owns the revenue stream for its line of business. This immediately reduces dependencies across tribes as well as competition for priorities. It also allows each tribe to focus on its own set of metrics. The teams within each tribe can now suggest OKRs for themselves that serve as leading indicators for only that tribe's strategic goals. These team-level OKR proposals travel up to tribe leadership and then back down to the teams, creating an alignment that has few, if any, dependencies outside of the tribe.

The autonomy of the tribes allows each to work on product planning in a way that differs from traditional roadmaps. Instead of committing to a set of features by a specific date, the tribe commits to a general direction of work that aligns with its top-level OKR goals. Any prioritization changes or rethinking of work deliverables are framed within the context of the tribe's OKRs and the general direction it has committed to for the current cycle. If a tribe, through feedback from its component teams, realizes they cannot achieve the product direction they've committed to, they use the collective evidence gathered by the teams to shift directions. They can have this level of agility explicitly because the teams have committed to customer behavior changes, not specific features.

Finally, the transparency in each tribe carries through to the learning work each component team does. They've set up research repositories to capture documents and quantitative data in a central place for each tribe that prevents inadvertent sharing but also encourages the use of a single source of data for any related conversations. Between this tool, a monthly release report, and a Slack channel used for sharing findings, the tribes manage what they're learning along the way, both reducing the risk of duplicating efforts and ensuring that any future learning activities take into consideration what's already been done.

Key Takeaways

1. Working with OKRs has implications not only for teams but for leaders, too. It's not enough to write them; you need to follow through and support your teams in doing the work necessary to achieve them.

2. The OKR process works if you let it. Leaders get anxious about new processes because it feels like they've lost control. Let the OKR process run and learn from each iteration— making it better every cycle.

3. Learning work makes OKRs successful. Do everything you can to ensure everyone in the company knows how to do research and is encouraged to use it regularly.

4. Data is the lifeblood of a learning organization. Everyone needs access to it without obstacles. Make it easy and obvious how to find out what customers are doing at any given moment.

5. To enable OKR success, leaders need to foster a psychologically safe culture where learning is celebrated at every turn. Teams should feel comfortable asking questions, making mistakes, and sharing and testing their ideas.

6. Cultures develop according to the leaders that shape them. To have teams that embrace learning and experimentation, leaders need to model behaviors that reflect those values.

Chapter 15

Managing Up, Changing Responsibilities

OKRs change the game. We've said it a lot, and by now, you know that well enough. As with any game, when the rules change, you need to change how you manage the players. Leaders at the top of the organization play key roles in this. Middle managers—leaders of teams, departments, functional specialists, and business units—are just as important. What's more, they probably have an even harder job. Pick your metaphor—they're the glue between the layers, they're the protein in the middle of the sandwich—the point is that they face pressures from every side. Middle managers are the ones on the ground with their teams, guiding them on the day-to-day while also playing ball with the leaders above them. They need to bridge the gaps so that their teams stay **aligned** and **focused**; they must encourage and create **transparency** to keep leaders informed and supportive. They need to make plans, manage work, and encourage **agility**. OKRs amplify the need for all of these things, and that changes how middle managers do their jobs.

The way we see it, the change falls into three categories: managing up to senior leadership, giving managers new responsibilities, and adjusting the criteria for evaluating employee performance. There's a lot to cover here, so let's get to it.

How to Manage Up When Using OKRs

Regardless of how well-intentioned or supportive of OKRs your leaders may be, organizational change is a big task, and it's challenging at every level. Those of you in managerial roles must be comfortable managing up—by which we mean working effectively with the leaders above you to get the support you need to implement OKRs successfully. Here's what we recommend.

Tie Everything Back to OKRs

It's nearly inevitable that from time to time, your bosses will make specific requests: *We need to add this new thing to our list of service offerings. I need you to get more billable hours from the employment law practice. I want you to build this video filter feature.* In more traditional environments, that might be the end of the conversation. Boss says *jump*, you say *how high?* In organizations operating with OKRs, though, every activity and decision should be tied back to the high-level OKRs.

Ideally, your leaders should do this for you—tell you a compelling story that makes a clear connection between the OKRs and their decisions and directives. When they don't, and if you feel comfortable, try to create a conversation that helps them do this. It might look a little like this:

> BOSS: *"I want you to build this video filter feature for our app."*

> YOU: *"Terrific idea, boss. Which of our OKRs will that help achieve?"*

Now, if your boss tells you a compelling story that makes sense, great! Remind them of the OKR process to validate the idea: "We'll add it to our to-do list, run some experiments, and make sure it's going to deliver the behavior change we're looking for."

If, however, your boss doesn't or can't tell a compelling story, or doesn't tie it back to a higher-level OKR, ask some more questions to try to help create that story together with your boss. After all, the request is coming in for a reason. Your first job is to try to understand the reason.

If, after those conversations, you can't find the connection to your OKRs, you might have to do some more nudging:

- "If we can't tie it to our OKRs, it's hard to justify prioritizing it."
- "If we go ahead with it, which of our key results or activities are you OK abandoning?"
- "If we don't work on those activities, here's what will change about our targets and activities for the rest of the quarter. Here's how much we'll need to reduce them."

Your role in these conversations is to make sure your boss understands the consequences of the new work they're asking you to do. Your work is constrained by the number of people you employ and the amount of time you have to do the work. There's only so much a team can get done in a specified timeframe. If your boss requests new work in the current timebox, something needs to come out. As the saying goes, you can't fit 10 pounds of sh*t in a five-pound bag. That's how time works.

You have another role in these conversations too, which is to do everything you can to allow your team to **focus** on their OKRs. When something the boss wants done threatens to take your team off-track, use the structure that OKRs provide to express what's most important and maintain the focus and alignment of your team.

Tell Your Story Constantly

In the same way leaders need to tell compelling stories about their directives and decisions, you need to tell compelling stories about your work to them at all times. That's a key part of the trust equation with OKRs. You get more **autonomy** to make decisions and drive your own goals and work; leaders need to hear how it's all going. It's trust built on **transparency**.

Thankfully, OKRs provide many opportunities for transparency. Use them. Use your regularly scheduled check-ins. Use your knowledge management systems. Use your communication channels. Send a quick update when you've learned something new, made a different decision based on evidence, or realized a change needed to be made. It's as simple as an email saying, "Hey, you asked us to focus on this. Here's what we've been doing, and here's how it's going." Make this a habit.

When you proactively communicate the story of what's going on with your work, you and your leaders can address problems sooner and more easily. And your leaders are more likely to give you the support and tools you need to succeed.

Practice Customer-centricity with Your Leaders

The best way to receive support from your leaders is to build trust with them, but that trust doesn't always come easily, especially if you're just starting to build more transparency into your processes. It may help to think about your leaders as customers. (Everyone has a customer! Your bosses are probably some of your most important customers.) OKRs are all about customer-centricity, and when you're asking your leaders for resources or sign-offs, they are your customers in those moments. You want them to buy into your work and give you the resources you need, so think about what *they* need.

What are they trying to accomplish? What is their mission as a leader? What problems are they concerned with right now? What do they need in order to succeed in their job? How can you make them successful?

They have a different vantage point than you do, and they're working with a different set of information. They might be on the hook for something that's not clear to you. Try to see things from their perspective and see how that informs your approach. If you can connect your work, or the specific request you're making, to the things they're concerned about and to how you can help them meet their commitments, you might just get that OK. You might even gain their trust.

For example, if you're managing a small business unit and you find yourself short-staffed, you may make a request to hire more people. How does that tie into your OKR? Can you weave together a story that connects your request to your OKR to your boss' goals? It could look something like this:

> *"I'd like to hire two more software engineers and one more designer. The increase in staff will allow us to increase our Q3 OKR targets by 20%, which ladders up to a 50% increase in the business unit's Q3 targets."*

Changing the Responsibilities of Middle Managers

In a typical organization, a manager's job is to be a sort of middleman. Managers turn strategic direction from the top into a list of tasks, assign those tasks and responsibilities to their teams, and then manage the work. They make sure everyone is getting their work done well, on time, and on budget, and those are their measures of success. When OKRs come into the picture though, the measures of success change. Instead of the binary "this got done or it didn't," success is now measured in terms of results: *Did our actions change customer behavior in a specific, measurable, and positive way?* In this world, the taskmaster part of the manager's job goes out the window. Instead of assigning work to your teams, your teams determine what's best for them to work on.

Don't lament this. Celebrate it. OKRs don't get rid of the value of managers or their skills. Rather, OKRs change managers' responsibilities in a way that allows you to use your skills in new ways, helping you truly lead instead of just (micro-)manage.

So, if you're not telling people what to do, what are your new responsibilities as a manager?

- Ensuring the team's OKRs and work are aligned with strategic direction, and clarifying the team's purpose
- Setting guidelines and constraints around the team's scope of work

- Clearing the team's path of organizational hurdles and ensuring they have what they need to do their best work
- Making key decisions when the team needs guidance

Ensuring Strategic Alignment and Clarifying the Team's Purpose

A friend of ours used to run an entrepreneurship course at a university in Kent, England—one of those courses where students form teams, come up with an idea for a business or service, and then iterate their idea and try to launch their business by the end of the semester.

One semester, he had a team whose vision was to create a healthy food delivery service for students. They dove in with this strategy, conducted customer research, and ran experiments. Of course, they iterated, too. When the end of the semester came around, they'd fully pivoted and launched an alcohol delivery service. Why? Because—surprise, surprise—that's what the student population told them that they wanted. They were iterating in the heat of the moment and following what they were learning from the market, and as a result, they entirely lost sight of their original vision and strategy.

We see this all the time. And though it may sound like the team was being customer-centric, the goal of customer-centricity isn't just to give people anything they want; it's to solve a problem or serve a need within the scope of your vision and within the mission of your organization. It's important for teams to have somebody keeping that vision top of mind so they can bring everyone back and say, "We *know* students want alcohol. (We probably didn't need to do research to figure that out.) But that's not what we're doing here. We're trying to prove that there is a desire for healthy eating among students that can be fulfilled in a fun, efficient, and cost-effective way." Until your team has completely disproved their original strategy or vision, it's their job to figure out a way to deliver the vision in a way that also serves the needs of the customer.

Ensuring clarity of purpose is a big part of your job because it allows the teams to better assess if their work is on track. Every time the team starts to drift off course, it's your responsibility as a manager to steer them back in the right direction. And remember, that direction is defined by their OKRs. That's your—and their—guiding light. Keep coming back to that.

Setting Guidelines and Constraints Around the Team's Scope of Work

Managing the scope of your team's work with clear strategic direction is another key element of your team's success. There are an infinite number of ways, with infinite levels of complexity, to solve a problem. This can feel like an exciting opportunity for teams who are particularly creative, and it can feel overwhelming for others who are used to the traditional idea of working until something is "done." But when you're working with outcomes, as you are in OKRs, the work is never done. You're constantly iterating and improving as your customers and their behaviors change, always trying to get better results.

Because of that, it's better to deliver value in smaller batches, with consistency over time, than to swing for the fences with long-term, ambitious, or wildly creative projects. That is a significant mindset shift for many teams, though, and they need managers to help reiterate the shift in the form of guidelines and constraints.

A few years ago, an executive we worked with at CapitalOne, a large U.S. bank, had a team come to her asking for $20 million to implement a big, comprehensive IT system over the course of two years. They had compelling reasons and a persuasive story. They demonstrated the logic behind the idea. Still, $20 million is a lot to ask for.

"It sounds like a valuable project," she told them. "I'm going to give you 25% of what you're asking for: $5 million to get started. In six months, show me your results. Show me that you've created actual value with that money—not just that you've built stuff for six months. If you do that, I'll give you the next $5 million for the next six months."

Which they did, and she did. They got their $20 million over the course of the two years, and they delivered value continuously.

This was a canny leadership tactic. By putting some constraints on the project, she ensured the team focused on value delivery at every phase of the project, instead of just at the end. It also forced the team to manage their scope so that they didn't get bogged down by the size of the project right out of the gate. In addition, this constraint forced the team to rethink their plans. Rather than focusing on delivering a specific set of features each quarter, they were forced to figure out how to deliver working slices of the project, one increment at a time. Plus, their customers would begin seeing the benefits in the first six months, not two years later.

As an added bonus, the usage of these first versions of the product would inform subsequent work, ensuring the team was always working on a service that was valuable to the end customer.

Clearing Organizational Hurdles

The constraints that you put in place as a manager to keep your team aligned and on mission are one thing. They're important and necessary limits. The obstacles that arise inside organizations that impede progress are a different thing altogether. As Astro Teller said, when you want teams to do something, you need to make that thing the path of least resistance. Identifying and then removing obstacles is a critical part of the manager's job.

In the case of OKRs and customer-centric ways of working, you want to pay particular attention to the obstacles that stand in the way of learning work, data access, and team autonomy. Your job as a manager is to make it possible for your teams to make rapid forward progress toward their goals.

Be your team's champion, help clear up any questions with other leaders or teams, and try to smooth out the path for their work to happen. Make sure your people have the tools they need, the access they require, and the rewards that motivate them to do their best work.

Josh remembers a leader who modeled this kind of support for him:

At my first job on Wall Street, I was hired as a design manager at a brokerage. Not long after I started, one of the designers on my team asked if she could have a digitizing tablet, which was what we used at the time to make hand-drawn computer graphics. I said "yes," and when I asked the other designers on the team, two more people said they could use them, too.

Then, I realized that I'd committed to an expensive purchase—and it was one of the first things I'd done on the job. I was worried about what my boss would think. I ended up editing the order so that we could buy mid-priced tablets instead of the expensive ones my team had asked for.

What I didn't realize was that my purchase request would be routed electronically not just to my boss, but, because it was expensive, to the CEO as well. I found out because moments after I'd submitted the purchase request, the CEO called me. This was my first conversation with him since I'd started at the company.

"Why are you buying these tablets?" he said. I didn't know him very well yet, and I thought I was in trouble.

"Well, my designers need them to do their jobs more effectively," I said hesitantly.

"No," he said. "Why are you buying the cheap ones? Why aren't you buying the top-of-the-line models?"

The top-of-the-line models were about seven times more expensive than the already expensive mid-priced ones I'd requested! But the cost didn't matter to him. What mattered was that his team had the best equipment they could have so they could do the best work possible.

You might not have a CEO who's excited about spending thousands of dollars on premium-grade equipment for your team. In fact, you may not even have an easy time getting approval for $50 Starbucks gift cards for customer interviews. But as managers, it's your responsibility to advocate for your team and convince senior leaders of the need for these resources. Whether it's equipment, access to internal systems, or subscriptions to tools, make sure—to the best of your ability—that your team has exactly what they need to do their best work.

Helping the Team Make Key Decisions

The funny thing about doing outcome-based work is that everybody expects the data from research to show decisive results, and it rarely does. You don't often learn that an idea is definitively right or wrong; it's typically somewhere in the middle. That can make it hard for teams to decide how to proceed. Even when they go back and get more data, the results still may not be clear. But the team needs to proceed in some way.

As a manager, it's your job to be the decisive voice. Come in and break the deadlock. Keep the team moving. Bias them toward action. Keep the strategy in mind, and if there's more than one option on the table, it's your responsibility to make the strategic call.

Keep in mind, your decision (or your team's) is not the end-all, be-all. Like everything else, it's a hypothesis, and you can certainly pivot in the future. But keep moving forward. When your team gets stuck, they should know to look to you for help. Make the call, then be prepared to defend it.

One more thing to remember: Whatever decision your team makes may only survive until the end of your next timebox. Once new evidence comes in, you may pivot once again. Reminding your team of that as you help them make a decision reinforces the psychological safety required for OKRs to succeed.

Adjust Performance Management Criteria

One of the most consistent questions that we hear about OKRs is whether they should be used in performance management, and if so, how?

Let's start our answer with this: **Do not create individual OKRs and then use them for individual performance management.**

Remember at the beginning of the book when we said that there are no firm and fixed rules about OKRs? Well, this might be one of the few firm and fixed rules about OKRs. We've never seen this work, and we've never spoken to anyone who has seen this work either. We have, however, spoken to many, many, *many* people who have seen organizations try to do this and fail. *Don't do this.*

Let's talk about why.

If you ask your teams to work differently but reward them for working in the old ways, they will inevitably optimize for what gets them paid. This will be the death knell of your organizational transformation. But if you believe strongly in this new customer-centric way of working, then the way you measure your employees' work performance and success needs to change as well.

OKRs work when they **create alignment**. In practice, this means that we want everyone pulling in the same direction and pulling together. One of the (many) things that get in the way is misaligned incentives. You see this whenever you encounter a high-pressure car salesman, for example. That one salesman is trying to make a sale and earn himself a commission. The company may have other objectives, though, like customer satisfaction. And really, what's less satisfying than battling a high-pressure salesman?

So, inside any organization, you need to work hard to make sure that your incentives are driving people together rather than creating conflict. When you create individual OKRs for people, you immediately increase the number of goals and the number of incentives that people have. This will pretty much guarantee that people will have conflicting and misaligned incentives. They'll have personal goals. They'll have team goals. Those two sets of goals, at some point, will be likely to conflict.

So don't do this. Don't create OKRs at the individual level. Instead, keep OKRs at the team level. Then, refer to these team-level OKRs when setting individual performance management goals. Expect people to orient their work toward those OKRs, then evaluate their contribution to them.

Now obviously, a team might fail to achieve their OKRs, even if every single member of the team does an excellent job. So when you're considering individual performance, remember that distinction, and make sure that you're evaluating how well the individual performs, rather than penalizing them for things that were beyond their control.

One way to evaluate individual performance in the OKR world is to use the seven key principles of OKRs: focus, autonomy, alignment, accountability, transparency, agility, and customer-centricity. Below, we share some guidance on how to do this.

1. **Focus, Accountability, and Prioritization:**
    *Evaluate how well the individual used
    their time in service of the OKR.*

    How do they choose what to work on and what not to? Do they become distracted by other projects or by personal interests, or are they disciplined in their use of time? When faced with conflicting priorities, are they able to choose wisely? When choosing tasks to work on, you want the team members to consistently refer to the OKR that the work supports.

    Of course, using OKRs doesn't mean that people spend 100% of their time on OKR-related work. There's always important work that's not specifically OKR-related. The question you want to ask is: How well does this person balance the conflicting demands on their time?

2. **Agility and Learning:**
   *Evaluate how well a person incorporates learning
   activities into their work cycle and how well they use
   evidence to inform their work and make decisions.*

   How much contribution does a person make to their
   team's learning activities? How well do they refer to
   what they've learned to help the team decide what
   to work on and how to work on it? Since empowered
   teams with OKR goals must build learning into their
   work, you need to make sure that this work is happening and that each individual is both contributing and
   leveraging these activities.

   If teams are gathering evidence, how well do the
   individuals use that evidence? Why do they spin up a
   project? Why do they kill an idea? Why did they decide
   to work on a specific thing? Do they know? They
   should. And they should be able to point to data that
   justifies their efforts—both the big efforts and the
   small ones.

   Finally, how willing are they to change course in
   the face of evidence? Do they fall in love with their
   ideas, or do they fall in love with the problem, solving
   the problem, and the results they're trying to achieve?

3. **Alignment, Autonomy, and Collaboration:**
   *Evaluate how well individual team members
   collaborate and communicate with one another.
   Evaluate how well they balance personal
   needs, local interests, and company mission.*

Alignment and autonomy are challenging properties to maintain. They are in constant tension with each other. Add in the needs of the individuals on the team, and you have many forces at play, all with the potential to pull the team apart or to push them out of alignment with the organization's high-level goals.

How well does a given person manage these competing forces? How well can they harness their own strengths and abilities and put them to the service of the team and the organization?

Individual heroism is yesterday's news. Individuals don't deliver world-class, high-performance, scalable, secure, well-written, or well-designed products and services. Teams do. Successful teams collaborate and communicate well. This is what allows them to work with a high degree of autonomy. They create the psychological safety that enables everyone to share ideas and communicate transparently about why certain decisions were made and others were rejected. Highly collaborative teams build their own vocabulary to drive efficiency and can increasingly anticipate one another's needs as they work together.

4. **Transparency and Knowledge-Sharing:**
    Evaluate how well individual team members share information with one another, as well as their ability to share information effectively across the organization.

How well does an individual share their knowledge? How willing are they to be radically transparent about their work, their progress, and the places where they're struggling and might need help?

How well do they help the team work with other teams and people in the larger organization?

Teams don't work on their OKRs in a silo. They work with other teams. Sometimes the information they learn in the course of their work is relevant and helpful to colleagues across the organization. Other times, teams make decisions that people outside of the team should know about.

5. **Customer-centricity:**
   Evaluate how effectively an individual works to understand the customer and their experiences and serve their needs.

Teams that care about hitting their OKR goals care about their customer—whoever that customer is. They know the customer because they speak with them regularly. They empathize with their needs and continuously confirm that those needs are being met. Leadership and organizational design expert David Marquet stresses the need to push day-to-day decision-making down to the people in your organization who are closest to the customer. On any given day, there shouldn't be anyone closer to the customer than the team working to serve that customer.

So, do the individuals on the team share a passion for customer success? Do they orient their work around their customers' needs? Are they motivated to learn and understand? Are they effective advocates for customer needs?

Change Requires Change

This is by no means a complete list of potential performance management criteria for individuals working in an OKR-driven organization. There are many other things you could evaluate. The main point here is that OKRs will likely challenge your current performance management system. We hope this list inspires conversations within your organizations and with your HR leaders about how to ensure you're not only writing great OKR goals, but you're also creating the performance management systems that incentivize a culture where OKRs thrive. In all likelihood, you'll need to rewrite some job descriptions. The impact of OKRs across the organization is not small.

This is where these transformations truly come to a head. With almost every organization we've ever worked with, changing performance management criteria has always been one of the last considerations. In fact, most organizations don't think about this key aspect of their customer-centric transformation until it's too late.

Key Takeaways

1. Middle managers are vital for bridging the gaps between teams and leaders so that teams stay aligned and focused and leaders stay informed and supportive. OKRs amplify these needs, which changes how middle managers do their jobs.

2. Under OKRs, middle managers no longer set tasks and run point. Their job is to align their team's work with the organization's strategy, set scope-of-work constraints, clear the team's path of hurdles, ensure they have what they need to do their best work, and make key decisions when needed.

3. Using OKRs in organizations is hard at all levels and requires a lot of coordination and communication. Middle managers may need to manage up to their leaders—by tying everything back to OKRs—so that leaders understand how their decisions impact the team's ability to achieve their goals *and* teams get the support they need.

4. In most organizations, performance management criteria are tied to whether or not teams achieve their goals. Since the kinds of goals teams work toward change with OKRs, managers (and their leaders) need to decouple performance evaluation from goal completion entirely.

5. Instead, teams should be evaluated on behaviors and qualities that are important for guiding success with OKRs—things like prioritization, learning, collaboration, knowledge-sharing, evidence-based decision-making, and customer understanding.

Chapter 16

Scaling OKRs

How do you implement OKRs at scale?

Most organizations that adopt OKRs do so because someone in the organization sees the benefits that are possible *if only the whole company could work this way.* It's a tempting vision, worth pursuing but with the right timeline expectations. Operationalizing OKRs at scale across a large organization can often take years.

There's no single path to change, of course. With OKRs, though, there are some patterns that we've seen that work well, and in this chapter, we're going to share them with you.

Build from a Strategic Foundation

At the risk of repeating ourselves: It all starts with strategy.

Without a clear organizational strategy, you'll struggle to build alignment with OKRs. This is true at the team level, the business unit level, and it's especially true at the organizational and leadership levels.

If you want to drive alignment and focus in your organization, you first need to answer the question: What's the focus? What should we align around?

Strategy is an alignment tool. It's an anchor for all your OKR efforts to attach to. It's a focus tool. It tells teams what's important and what's not. It gives direction and provides guardrails. It allows people to figure out what to work on and what *not* to work on. When teams understand the strategy thoroughly, they think more deeply about how the work they do can help bring that strategy to fruition. Most importantly, strategy gets the entire organization pulling in the same direction.

Align. Don't Cascade.

In Chapter 4, we wrote about strategy and how to get started. In Chapters 5 and 6, we wrote about how to create OKRs from strategy. And finally, in Chapter 7, we wrote about the importance of creating OKRs from strategy in both a top-down and bottom-up way. We're not going to repeat ourselves here. We bring all this up because there's one really important caution to keep in mind when it comes to scaling OKRs: The bigger your organization, the more careful you should be to avoid "cascading" OKRs.

What do we mean by this? Well, there's a school of thought in the OKR community that recommends "cascading" OKRs. In this process, management sets a high-level goal and then prescribes how that goal cascades down through the organization's individual business units and teams. Essentially, leadership is dictating goals from the top. This central planning approach has a surface appeal. It seems simple and fast. It allows a relatively small number of leaders to maintain a lot of control and make goal-setting decisions quickly. There's a problem though: It rarely works.

We wrote about the importance of a top-down and bottom-up approach in Chapter 7. The bigger your organization, the more important and complex this becomes. When your organization grows, leaders get farther away from customers. This is natural and inevitable. It's also a big risk. OKRs, if used correctly, ask the people who are closest to the customer to be deeply involved in the goal-setting process. It gives them ownership of their work because they chose it and it's within their sphere of influence. This taps a critical resource in the organization and brings it into the planning process. Cascading OKRs ignore this source of knowledge. Planning is invariably worse for it.

So, instead of cascading, think of scaling your OKRs like a family tree. Every OKR needs to have a parent. A child OKR should clearly support the parent OKR. This has three main benefits:

1. Every goal set at every level of the organization supports the higher purpose. You can trace it all the way up to the strategy.
2. Every goal has an owner. Owners drive accountability.
3. Leaders still get a top-down discipline while allowing for flexibility and creative contribution from the bottom up.

Being able to trace the "lineage" of each OKR ensures we don't have any orphan goals floating around in the company. It ensures each person, team, team of teams, business unit, and department is pulling in the same direction—toward the shared strategic goal. It also provides a level of control over an entire portfolio of work. We can quickly see how well a team of teams is progressing toward their goal as well as the impact they're having on the broader organization, for example. This is particularly helpful as OKRs are scaled up into the hundreds and thousands of teams. At the highest levels of an organization, it also gives us a clearer sense of how much of the work we're doing is actually moving us forward toward the strategy—a key metric in operational efficiency.

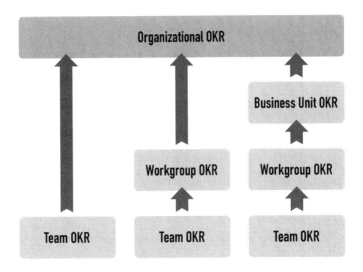

Important note: The parent/child relationship described here applies to the entire OKR, objective included. It's easier for teams to ignore the qualitative objective in favor of the often more obvious numerical key result. Avoid this as you scale. Each team should understand their alignment from both a qualitative and quantitative perspective. They should understand that, regardless of where they sit in the organization, they make someone's life better, easier, more efficient. Forgetting to scale your objectives puts teams at risk of drifting away from the strategic goal.

Once leadership has finished setting the high-level OKRs for the organization, ask every department and team to set their own team-level OKRs. The constraint that they must respect here is simple: Lower-level OKRs must support the higher-level objectives set "above" each team in the organizational hierarchy.

Another important note: To help drive broad adoption and usage of OKRs across the organization, every team and leader at every level of the business should write their own OKRs. This activity should not be outsourced to a subordinate. Every time someone in the organization (including the C-suite) needs to write OKRs they're learning more about the process and how it impacts their sphere of influence. This learning-by-doing should lead to greater empathy across the company not only for the customers we serve but also for the OKR process itself.

The Old-School Boss

Jeff once worked for a stodgy, older boss on the verge of retirement. He was as old-school as they come. When Jeff approached him after a year of work for his annual review, his boss said, "If I'm still paying you, you're doing a good job."

Uh, thanks?

For Jeff's boss the only thing that mattered was money. Similarly, many leaders see the only important goal for the company as short-term revenue. If we're hitting our numbers, we're doing fine.

As companies grow and scaling OKRs becomes more complicated, there can be a temptation to short-circuit the entire process and just give everyone the same revenue goal. As Jeff's boss would have likely said, "If the customers are paying us, we're doing a good job."

OKRs at scale are indeed complicated to manage, but giving the entire organization a revenue goal doesn't solve the problem. It just sets up the majority of your teams to fail. As we've said before, there are many customer behaviors between "deliver your work product" and "make money." Each team in your company takes care of some part of that customer journey. And each of those teams has its own customer to consider. It's just not always the end purchaser (i.e., the person paying us).

By optimizing the customer behavior at each stage, your teams are improving the leading indicators that ultimately drive revenue. Would you ask the cybersecurity team to hit a revenue number? What about the in-house legal and compliance team? You shouldn't. Their work leads customers to behave in certain ways that, if successful, will drive up revenue or drive down costs. But assigning them a specific portion of that revenue sets them up to fail. They can't directly influence it.

Teams Can Share OKRs

What if you have 500 teams? 5,000 teams? Does each team need its own OKR? The short answer is no. At scale, you'll see many teams with dependencies on one another. Some of those teams can share goals. These teams may still have some goals they can achieve on their own, but the dependencies mean that their overall success is linked to their collaboration with other teams. In these cases, these teams should share the same OKR. This arrangement might be short-term, lasting only a quarter or two, or it might last longer. This would depend on the scope of the work and the pace of progress toward the shared goal.

For example, in an online checkout process there can be many teams responsible for each part of the customer journey—the product detail page, adding to cart, signing in, payment, and post-purchase customer support. Each of those teams can optimize its unique part of the process, but the overall goal is shared: getting customers through the purchase process successfully and quickly. In this case, these teams might share an OKR designed to optimize the entire purchase journey.

Allowing teams to share OKRs helps reduce the occurrence of the main anti-patterns of scaled OKR implementation: hyperlocal optimization. One team might work hard to hit their key results but at the same time, the work they're doing might inadvertently hamper another team's progress. In other words, the work of these two teams are dependent on each other in some way, but the teams aren't coordinating or communicating. They may not even be aware of the dependency between them. Without a shared goal or process to communicate about their progress toward that goal, the first team will just drive forward. After all, they're on the hook for their own goals, not those of their colleagues. Sharing an OKR brings the kind of transparency required for dependent teams to work successfully together.

To get to a shared OKR goal for dependent teams, we first identify a set of teams who will be dedicated to the same goal and have them create their OKRs together, as a team of teams, to set their shared objectives and key results. This team of teams is now on the hook, as a unit, for these goals. Once approved, the team of teams now has alignment and shared success criteria.

TEAM OF TEAMS

Objective:
The simplest checkout process in the online grocery business by the end of 2025.

Key Result: Increase the number of customers successfully completing checkout on first attempt by 75%.

Key Result: Customer checkout time is reduced by 50% on average.

TEAM 1	TEAM 2	TEAM 3
Objective: Clear and compelling product detail pages by Q3	**Objective:** Seamless sign-inprocess for existing customers by Q3.	**Objective:** Easiest way to pay for groceries online by Q3.
Key Result: Increase percentage of customer visits that results in product added to cart by 55%	**Key Result:** Reduce customer failed authentication attempts during checkout process by 95%.	**Key Result:** Reduce number of abandoned carts due to payment issues by 90%.

In this example, the overall goal is in the top box. There are three teams supporting this OKR with their own lower-level goals that serve as leading indicators for the overall goal.

Individual team-level OKRs still makes sense.

This doesn't necessarily mean that each team doesn't have its own team-specific goals to achieve. In fact, one of the first things to ask the component teams for is a set of OKRs to function as leading indicators of the group's overall goals. In this way, each team is working toward a goal they can influence directly but they're doing so with:

- A clear line of sight of the overall goal they're trying to achieve
- A transparent view into how their work is impacting other teams in the group
- The awareness that if the OKRs they've chosen don't have the impact they predicted on the group's goals, they'll need to adjust their goals.

Everything else stays the same.

At scale, this approach reduces the overall number of goals and activities a company needs to track. This simplifies the management, review, and decision-making process for leaders. It makes operationalizing OKRs less onerous when dealing with very large organizations. The rest of the OKR process stays the same for the teams both for their individual as well as their shared OKRs.

Reconciling and Approving OKRs at Scale

Though teams should set their own OKR goals, leadership still needs to approve them—especially at scale. In addition, they need to reconcile them with all the other teams' goals across the entire business unit or organization. The individual teams have put together goals appropriate for their sphere of influence. Their leaders can see the broader forest for the trees and can help determine whether or not to approve the proposed OKRs and how to handle situations where they don't align well.

The key factor when you're seeking to scale the OKR process is speed. In a large organization, it may be tempting to create a process that involves careful review and approval at every level. We've certainly all seen how long "planning season" can last in big organizations. We've seen some companies take nearly all of Q4 and Q1 to make plans for the year. That's six months of planning!

The best way to move quickly is to push the power down into the organization. Set and communicate your strategy and the high-level OKRs. Then set a timebox. Give teams a few weeks to draft, review, reconcile, and approve their OKRs. Give managers the power and the trust to lead this work. Then get to work!

In large companies, the urge is to slow down. "We can't work like a startup!" To combat this, be rigid with the assigned timeboxes. The entire OKR-setting process should take no longer than a month once the high-level direction is communicated. Resist the temptation to break this time constraint. It's a forcing function to get through the goal-setting process and get on with the doing of the work.

"A month?! Are you crazy?! We can't get our cafeteria menus sorted in a month. How are we going to get goals done that quickly?" Remember (again), the longest you need to live with these commitments is one quarter. Bias for action and learning. Then, adjust course as new information comes in.

Expect OKR Rollouts to Take Years

Your OKR rollout will take time, between two and five years for large enterprise-level companies. Building a multi-year OKR deployment plan reduces the organization's ability to change tactics as new learnings come to light over those many years. As we do with any large-scale effort, whether it be a new initiative or policy or a new process rollout, we want to de-risk its rollout. We do that by treating the new idea like an experiment, starting small and stacking the deck with the best players we have to increase its likelihood of success.

Treat It Like an Experiment

Throughout this book, we've encouraged you to use OKRs to take a customer-centric view. Try to figure out what your customers need, then work in small batches—using an experimental mindset—to help them succeed. We want you to think about operationalizing OKRs at scale the same way.

When we roll out OKRs, the people in our organization are our customers. We can certainly bark orders at them, "Now you will use OKRs!" That's not very customer-centric, is it? If we instead took an experimental mindset, we'd approach the problem in a different way.

Experiments share one common attribute: They test our ideas in a way that is safe to fail. When we think about rolling out OKRs to a large organization, using an experimental approach allows us to accomplish the rollout in a series of small, safe-to-fail steps.

Starting small, rather than with a broad company-wide rollout, helps you identify—and smooth out—the obstacles to scaling. Many leaders are impatient and want to make big changes fast. "We have 500 teams!" We know; we hear you. But if you try to change all 500 of them overnight, you're taking a big risk. We've seen too many big-bang approaches fail and sour people on OKRs.

Early in the book, we said that the #1 rule of OKRs is that there is no #1 rule of OKRs. That means that every OKR implementation is different because every organization is different. To succeed then, you'll need to discover the best ways for *your organization* to use and scale OKRs.

How Infobip tested and learned their way to successful OKR deployment

Infobip's OKR story is one of perseverance and learning. Infobip started in 2006 as an SMS provider for one-time passwords. Since then, the company has grown significantly to over 3,400 employees on six continents. Infobip's focus today is to "democratize the communication between business and people" by making it easy for companies to interact with their customers through whatever channel makes the most sense.

Infobip has been working toward a broad, company-wide OKR implementation since 2019. After struggling with implementation for a few years, they restarted their efforts in 2022 and then again in 2023. Why keep trying if success has been so elusive? Mihael Matošević, head of planning and strategy development, shared with us that the team at Infobip holds a deep belief that, "OKRs are critical for driving cross-organizational alignment."

Infobip's CEO, Silvio Kutić, has championed the method for years and believes OKRs offer the best way to focus the organization and prioritize the most important things at any given time. Kutić also embraces the experimental mindset. Every time Kutić and senior leadership have set out to implement OKRs, they've made some mistakes, learned from those mistakes, and improved on them in the next rollout. For example, in 2019, during their first rollout, the teams essentially rebranded their existing production goals as OKRs. They set OKRs exclusively at the regional level but didn't go further down into the organization to ask for each local department's goals. Without that direct request and not realizing the difference between OKRs and other goal-setting methods, the regional teams set ineffective goals focused on features instead of outcomes.

In 2022, the company tried again. This time they built in the function of "OKR champions"—folks who were trained in OKRs and available to help every team in every region. The goal here was to offer local teams more support in their OKR journey. Each team now had a specific person they could go to for help with their goal-setting work. Though this helped move along implementation efforts, it wasn't enough. OKR champions were important, but they were just a small number of people—the rest of the staff didn't have adequate OKR training. This lack of understanding across the broader organization doomed this second effort to fail, as well.

Finally in 2023, Infobip put all their learnings into practice. The company built an education component, complete with a variety of training materials (printouts, videos, and modules provided by external vendors) that allowed every employee to learn about OKRs and the OKR tool that the company had selected to manage the OKR process. Leadership wanted to ensure everyone across the company had a baseline understanding of OKRs.

All of this has led to a new, quarterly focus on planning and prioritizing work. Infobip learned the hard way that you can't just say "Let's do OKRs!" and hope that everything falls into place. There's a significant amount of training, education, and support work needed to ensure success. Having put such robust training and support in place has borne fruit, as the teams in each region now not only provide quality OKRs on a quarterly basis but also have a clear sense of why they're being asked for these types of goals.

Keep the Experiment Transparent

A few years ago, we worked with a mid-level manager (let's call him Bob) who had finally convinced his leadership to build a cross-functional team that worked toward OKRs. They agreed to fly in team members from all over the world for one week. Bob was excited. The team holed up in a conference room (which they called the "war room") for a week. During that week they brainstormed their OKRs, identified their target audience, came up with solution hypotheses, designed an experiment, and even began designing some early solutions.

At the end of the week, the team emerged from the war room, triumphant, with a huge "ta-da!" They were so proud of their work and the way their team had collaborated to create that work. Then, they started to show off their design work and their plans for future work. To their dismay, though, they were met only with skepticism. Their colleagues and executive sponsors rejected their ideas.

Why did this happen? No one else in the organization saw the process. They didn't see how that one team had gotten to this point. They didn't know which ideas the team tried and rejected nor why the ideas were rejected. They hadn't seen the data that drove the team's initial decisions nor the iterations that the team had made. For all they knew, the team had just made everything up over the course of the week. By hiding away in the war room and not sharing their work with the rest of the organization, the team had failed to bring their colleagues along with them on their journey. Bob was not only discouraged but also received a negative review that quarter for a *lack* of collaboration.

What should Bob have done differently? First, he should have taken the team out of that war room and placed them in the most visible spot in the office. Their work should have covered the windows and walls. Their learnings should have been shared regularly—as an end-of-day "demo" activity. Any changes in direction based on new evidence should have been announced along with the rationale for the course correction. In short, the experiment should have been evident to all.

The moral of the story here is to ensure your pilot effort is visible to everyone. **Err on the side of radical transparency. Over-communicate. Don't wait to be asked.** Tell everyone what the team is doing, why it's doing it, and what the progress is—even on a daily basis. Your goal is to build support for the work you want to do *as you're doing it.*

If you're in the office, put the team in a central location everyone can see. Have them share frequently. Encourage them to make themselves available to answer questions. Post updates regularly through all communication channels. In short, show your work, regardless of whether it's good, bad, or otherwise. You want the process and experiment to be evident to everyone so, as you head into designing and deploying your work, your colleagues are aligned with you.

As you begin rolling out your pilot team's experiments, ensure they're not in a war room. Make the experiment public. Share its success metrics. Ask the team to work in a central location visible to as many people as possible. If they work remotely, ask them to provide daily updates through commonly used communication tools and channels. Ensure they're providing regular updates to anyone interested, celebrating their wins when they have them, and announcing their course changes when they occur. The last thing you want is to nail the OKR process with a pilot team and then, "ta-da!" roll it out to a skeptical organization that hasn't seen its previous success.

Start Small

Consider starting with just one team. That's really small, we know. If that's too small, consider a small group of teams or a small workgroup. Just keep the group small. And keep it focused. **Create one OKR: one objective and three key results.** Finally, keep the timeline short. **Start with one quarter.** Then, give these folks all the support they need to make OKRs successful in their specific context.

This pilot group will function like a minesweeper. They will be the first to find the critical organizational "landmines" that will make deploying OKRs at scale difficult. They'll run up against managers demanding traditional planning and roadmaps. They'll meet customers who want to know exactly what products and features are coming. They'll hear from skeptical executives who are resistant to change.

This is all data. Successful pilot teams generate data that you can use for learning. This small first step allows you to see the struggles you'll encounter with a broader rollout. **If you can figure out how to handle the issues that come up for one team, you can start to think about handling them for 10, 20, 100, and eventually 1,000 teams.**

This pilot team is your first OKR experiment. You're using it to mitigate risk and maximize your chances of success. This experiment will help you learn how to best staff for OKRs, support the process, and adjust your organizational systems—and even your organizational design—for a future where multiple teams work toward these customer-centric goals with great agility and focus. It's your first experiment but by no means the last. This mindset—that your OKR rollout is an ongoing series of experiments—is one of the most important things you can do to ensure your success.

How a large telecommunications company deployed a pilot team to figure out how to scale OKRs

We spoke with one of the biggest mass media and telecommunications companies based in the U.K. It has tens of thousands of employees, 10,000 in the central London office alone. In the past few years, the organization has been rolling out OKRs at scale, starting first with the London office. We spoke with the head of operations about the process. Though they've had their share of obstacles with the broader OKR rollout, the head of ops shared the specific experiments the company ran that ultimately made their scaled OKR journey successful.

1. *Quarterly Cycles:*
   Use the scaffolding you already have in place.

Before using OKRs, the company already had quarterly cycles in place as their standard check-in timeframes. Teams and leadership alike were used to them. When they began to work with OKRs, they decided to keep the same cycles. This reduced team confusion as they took on new ways to set goals. It also reduced the risk of any team going too far down the wrong path since, in a worst-case scenario, no team would spend more than 12 weeks chasing goals that didn't make sense. Though this may seem like a long time, in an enterprise setting, it often takes at least this long to collect the necessary feedback to determine whether or not a team is on track. By minimizing the number of changes the teams were taking on at the outset of using a new process, the operations team increased the likelihood of broad OKR adoption across the organization.

2. *Pilot Teams:*
   Test the process before scaling broadly.

Changing 10,000 people's goals is a daunting and risky endeavor. The ops team recognized this and started small by running a "process experiment"—rolling out OKRs to what they called a "pilot program." This pilot program was a small program of people, at least by their standards (only 600 people, led by six executives) and primarily comprised of software developers working on customer-facing products and services. Choosing a part of the business where OKRs would more likely find an easy fit further increased the company's chances of successful OKR adoption. This part of the organization was already familiar with the quarterly cycle. Even better, they had direct access to end customers, which made setting and measuring goals more accessible and more apparent.

The ops team's first big learning from the pilot effort came after they asked the teams in the pilot program to develop their own goals. This created alignment and focus at the individual team level; however, it didn't align any of the teams to the broader organizational strategy. Without a high-level top-down strategic direction to point to, each team did its own thing. After one quarter of working with a bottom-up OKR approach, the ops team realized that the head of operations we spoke with needed to go back to the leadership team and ask them to prepare their own goals, align among themselves, and then share their agreed-upon direction with the pilot teams. Once the leadership team had those high-level OKRs, the pilot teams could improve their own goals to align with the organization's strategic focus. This improved alignment allowed the pilot teams to focus on the work that was most important strategically, rather than who was "shouting the loudest" or on "zombie projects" that weren't going anywhere, as they called them.

Working with the pilot teams taught the company a lot about rolling out OKRs. For one, they learned that despite being relatively small and autonomous, the pilot teams were not, in fact, ready to work on their own right away. They needed specific direction and alignment coming from the top. The ops team adjusted and asked the leadership team to provide strategic direction and alignment for the pilot teams. This improved things, giving the company the sense it could start rolling out OKRs more broadly.

Though the pilot teams were indeed working well at that point, they still had enough doubts and challenges that required a lot of support and a high level of attention from the operations team to resolve. After attempting to add more teams to the rollout, the ops team realized they should have more thoroughly "de-bugged" the process with the pilot teams before beginning org-wide implementation.

Ultimately, using pilot teams allowed the company to de-risk the rollout of OKRs with a smaller group and learn from their mistakes before implementing the framework at scale.

Stack the Deck

Finally, as you decide who to put on this pilot team, consider stacking the deck. You want the effort to succeed, right? Then, you better **put your best folks on the challenge**. If anyone can make this work, it's them.

This isn't cheating. It's setting yourselves up for the best chance of success. You want to show the organization the benefits of this new way of working. So, choose people who are likely to succeed. At the same time, you know that this pilot will face obstacles—you just don't know *which* obstacles they'll encounter. Choose people who, when faced with obstacles, will be able to work their way through them. Finally, choose people who are interested in the experiment and motivated to succeed, learn, and share what they have learned. Their feedback will help simplify those things for future teams transitioning to OKRs.

How Metro built its "stacked" OKR pilot team

Metro AG, based in Düsseldorf, Germany, is a leading international food wholesaler, operating over 600 stores in 30 countries and employing more than 100,000 people. With an operation this big, Metro needs to be efficient, and the company relies on technology to achieve this goal. With food orders regularly exceeding a ton of noodles per day per store (that's not a euphemism—they literally sell 2,000 pounds of noodles daily) and as Europe's largest buyer of fish, Metro continuously strives to improve its operations. OKRs have been a big piece of that equation. We spoke with Timo Salzsieder, Metro's chief solutions officer, about how he's been using OKRs to drive the efficiency of their operations. Salzsieder's main goal in deploying OKRs was to move from success being measured as "done on time and budget" to "we moved an important business metric: revenue."

When starting to roll out OKRs across your organization, the teams implementing the framework first should consist of folks most likely to succeed with OKRs. If the goal is to bring a new way of working to the organization, proving the model with teams most likely to get it right means the new idea will get a chance to grow beyond the initial experiment. Salzsieder and the team at Metro did precisely that. Instead of rolling out OKRs to all 100,000 employees, or even the 4,000 who work in tech, they chose an initial group of six teams with 60 people. These were tech teams focused on e-commerce work who'd been immersed in agile ways of working before. They had members from every discipline needed to ship digital products, including product managers, scrum masters, full-stack engineers, data people, UX designers, and researchers.

As you read the description of Metro's early OKR experiments, you might say to yourself, "Well, if any teams have a chance of success with OKRs, it's going to be digital, agile, and cross-functional teams." That was precisely the point, and it allowed the company to show that OKRs can work for the organization before bringing everyone else on board.

They used short cycles—often no more than three months—to try new ideas, see how those ideas impacted worked, and then pivot based on what they learned.

As their success has grown, Metro increased the number of teams working with OKRs. To support those teams' OKR implementation, they held internal training sessions and began to certify "OKR Masters." These individuals have a deep understanding of the methodology and are charged with guiding, coaching, and unblocking teams as they work through their goals on a quarterly basis. At the time of this writing, Metro had nearly 250 teams working with OKRs, including finance and HR. The early experiments with the "stacked" teams provided the basis for how to train and grow the practice beyond e-commerce. Even with 250 teams actively working with OKRs, Metro has implemented the goal-setting framework with only about 20,000 people. However, given their success to date, they've been able to use the low-risk approach that drove their initial wins as a way to convince their board to start using OKRs as well.

OKR Support Is a Full-Time Job

Rolling out a new goal-setting framework to an entire organization is hard work. It requires ongoing effort. And it requires experience and expertise. As your pilot team works and learns, they will be creating valuable knowledge that you want to leverage. Most organizations that attempt to roll out OKRs recognize that this process of learning, capturing the learning, and sharing that learning is critical and requires people to do that work. This can be a group of coaches, managers, or a blend of the two.

At the big UK telecommunications company we mentioned earlier, for example, the head of operations told us that his team spent a lot of time during their OKR rollout working with teams to ensure the quality of the

OKRs they were writing. They monitored the OKRs each team wrote and worked with teams that needed support and improvement. Over time, they saw the OKRs getting better and better. Confident, they decided to focus on other things for a quarter, only to discover that the quality of OKRs started slipping without oversight and guidance. They put folks back on the job and immediately saw teams writing better OKRs again.

This is a general lesson for OKR support. You'll want to support your people because OKRs, while powerful, are also challenging. Coaching, whether from a dedicated OKR coach or a well-trained manager, is an important success factor.

OKR Tools

When you're a small organization, you don't need many OKR tools. A sheet of paper hanging on the wall will do. As you grow, though, tools to support OKRs become more critical. The right tool increases transparency and work quality.

Generally speaking, we're agnostic about tools. Use whatever works best for your team, organization, and culture. The right tool can make a big difference, though. The telecom company we've talked about in this chapter told us that they saw dramatic differences in the quality of the OKRs that teams created once they began using the right tool—and that this led to more success in their broader OKR rollout.

The team there told us that at the beginning of the company's OKR journey, the pilot teams often made features and other outputs part of their key results—we've already talked about why this is a problem. When they started using a better enterprise-wide tool, though, it had features that helped people write better goals. It asked questions that made it clear to the team that their answers (and, thus, their goals) didn't meet expectations. The tool's questions asked for outcomes, but the teams were using outputs. It was instantly evident that their OKRs had to change to get the right goals—ones focused on outcomes—in place and align the teams more effectively.

This prompting for outcomes-based goals also changed how the company's leadership assigned work to the pilot teams. Instead of telling them exactly what to do and how to do it, leadership left the execution up to the teams. After all, the goals were no longer about shipping a specific feature but were instead about changing the behavior of their customers. Leadership themselves didn't know how to drive those behavior changes; but they recognized that handing down lists of features wouldn't work anymore.

Finally, the tool the company chose to help with their OKRs gave leadership visibility into the quality of the OKRs being written as well as what work choices the teams were making to achieve the new goals. It highlighted which teams were doing good work and which needed more attention. The executive team now uses the tool to check on the performance of each business unit (rather than the individual employees). They're learning they've set too many goals, creating dependencies that have slowed the change teams down. This kind of transparency has continuously improved the company's OKR efforts.

Key Takeaways

1. OKRs at scale start from a strategic foundation. Without a clear strategy, large companies end up with OKRs that have no owners and don't align with the corporate direction, wasting effort on work that doesn't support the greater goal.
2. Don't cascade your OKRs down to your teams from the top. Set high-level goals and let the teams provide their own OKRs supporting the higher goal. Every goal should be traceable from the top to its place in the organization.
3. Every OKR must have a parent. The parent functions as a leading indicator for the goal above it. This includes the objective as well as the key results.
4. Build pilot teams to run OKR experiments before scaling to the entire organization. Keep the experiments transparent and use the evidence they provide to decide how to scale up further.
5. Support your scaled OKR rollout with people and tools. Teams can get started with relatively low amounts of support. But as the rollout increases, having OKR champions and proper tools ensures a smoother increase in the scope of the change.
6. Remember, change at scale takes years. This isn't something we deploy once to everyone and forget about. It requires repeated learning, iteration, and pivoting the approach as scale increases. Be patient.

Closing Words

Who does what by how much?

As with any idea worth implementing, the power of OKRs lies in its simplicity. But the core of this simple idea challenges more than a century of management canon, a canon forged in slower-moving, more predictable markets. The idea that drove early industrial success, "if you build it they will come," no longer applies. There's too much change, technological disruption, and geopolitical upheaval.

OKRs reflect the real-world uncertainty that we face in our work. We all have strong opinions, opinions based on our experience and expertise. We believe that we know how to solve our business problems and meet the needs of our customers. These opinions are risky, though. Hiding that risk behind the tools of command and control leadership—speculative requirements, opinion-based directives, and prescriptive solutions—reduces our chances of success.

When we instead focus on our customers' success, it forces us to take an outside-in perspective on our work. What's happening outside our organization? Why is it happening? How will we know it's getting better? These are our starting points when we use OKRs to focus on outcomes.

The most powerful predictors of success today are humility and curiosity. The organizations, leaders, and teams that will win are the ones willing to admit that they're making educated guesses about how to best serve their customers and then go out into the world to test their ideas. The leaders who can stand up in front of their people and admit, "I was wrong," will build cultures of learning and agility that are able to respond to anything the world throws at them.

Maybe it's a bit ambitious to believe that a simple goal-setting framework can make all of that happen. But hey, we're optimists. And we're rooting for you.

Jeff & Josh
jeff@gothelf.co
josh@seiden.co

Acknowledgments

As much as we might wish, no book writes itself. Neither do we, as writers, work by ourselves. We didn't invent OKRs; instead, we're building upon the work of many talented writers, thinkers, and business practitioners. We'd like to acknowledge the work of John Doerr, who brought OKRs into the mainstream conversation and ensured that the ideas pioneered by Andy Grove more than four decades ago continue to see the light of day. We'd be remiss if we didn't mention Christina Wodtke and her classic book *Radical Focus*. Her work has been a significant influence on our thinking.

Our work has been shaped by so many amazing lean, agile, and digital transformation practitioners that it would be hard to mention them all. Huge thanks to Jon Smart, Giff Constable, and Christina Wodtke (yep, again) for reading our early drafts and being both tough and kind with their critiques.

We're grateful for our thousands of students, who have challenged us to explain our ideas clearly and succinctly. We've been lucky to have amazing clients who support our work and from whom we've learned so much. We'd like to thank the folks who've been coming to our OKR Office Hours for their monthly conversations, questions, and insights.

We are grateful to the many people we spoke to who shared their stories with us, many of which became case studies in this book. Thanks to Anthony Coppedge, Ingrid Alga, Jacqueline de Goede, Andres Vinueza at Grupo Industrial Graiman, Line Krauss-Larsen, Peder Skou and Ann Kristin Drevdal from Gyldendal, Mihael Matošević and Marin Bezić from Infobip, Shiren Vijiasingam at Instructure, Matthew Hayto at International Rescue Committee, Timo Salzsieder at Metro AG, Hugo Froes and Timo Bolse from OLX, Daniel Booth at Tesco, and Brett Knowles of Pm2 Consulting for sharing their thoughts and time with us.

Beyond the inspiration and foundational material, there is the team behind the creation of the book itself. Marjie Shrimpton played a tremendous role in weaving together much of our early material into an initial draft and helping us bring a second revision in on time. We're hugely grateful to her for pushing us forward and ensuring we stayed on topic. Cathy Yardley was a huge help with her late-game editorial support. The entire team at Arcbound has been a massive help in building the community and buzz around the launch of the book. We're proud to call them partners on this journey. Our longtime book design collaborator, Jennifer Blais, once again made the book look amazing. And, finally, Aida Perez for ensuring all the trains were on track and on time. We couldn't have done it without any of you.

Individually, Jeff would like to acknowledge that once again it's been an absolute pleasure writing a book with Josh (it's our third time!). A partnership like this is rare. To have it last more than 15 years and result in so many great successes over the years is something I'm truly lucky to have, and I don't take it for granted. My family—Carrie, Sophie, and Grace—once again let me disappear into lengthy "writing holes" to make this book a reality, and for their never-ending support and encouragement, I am forever grateful.

Josh would like to acknowledge Jeff. Every time we write a book together, we vow never to do it again, and yet somehow, here we are again. And once again, it reminds me why I love working with Jeff. When people ask me for career advice, I often tell them about our working partnership. Here's what I say: Find someone you trust, with whom you share values, and who complements your skills. Jeff makes up for my flaws, and I'm very grateful for that. This book was created through much chaos, so I'd like to thank my builder, Roger Contreras, my architect, Angie Hunsaker, and my next-door neighbors for putting up with me. I'd like to thank my mom, a model of love, perseverance, strength of conviction, and independence. And, of course, George, AJ, Naomi, and most of all, Vicky.

Resources

OKRs

Doerr, John. *Measure What Matters: How Google, Bono, and the Gates Foundation Rock the World with OKRs.* Portfolio, 2018.

Hellesoe, Natalija, and Mewes, Sonja. *OKRs at the Center: How to Design, Launch and Evolve Objectives & Key Results for Effective Strategy Execution.* Independently published, 2021.

Niven, Paul R., and Ben Lamorte. *Objectives and Key Results: Driving Focus, Alignment, and Engagement with OKRs.* Wiley, 2016.

Wodtke, Christina. *Radical Focus: Achieving Your Most Important Goals with Objectives and Key Results.* Cucina Media, 2016.

Learning from Customers

Constable, Giff. *Talking to Humans: Success Starts with Understanding Your Customers.* Self-published, 2014.

Constable, Giff. *Testing with Humans: How to Use Experiments to Drive Faster, More Informed Decision Making.* Self-published, 2021.

Gothelf, Jeff, and Seiden, Josh. *Lean UX: Designing Great Products with Agile Teams*. O'Reilly Media, 2022.

Patton, Jeff, with Peter Economy. User Story Mapping: Discover the Whole Story, Build the Right Product. O'Reilly Media, 2014.

Portigal, Steve. *Interviewing Users: How to Uncover Compelling Insights*. Rosenfeld Media, 2013.

Torres, Teresa. *Continuous Discovery Habits: Discover Products that Create Customer Value and Business Value*. Product Talk LLC, 2021.

Outcomes

Penna, Robert M. *The Nonprofit Outcomes Toolbox: A Complete Guide to Program Effectiveness, Performance Measurement, and Results*. John Wiley & Sons, 2011.

Seiden, Joshua. *Outcomes Over Output: Why Customer Behavior Is the Key Metric for Business Success*. Sense & Respond Press, 2019.

"W.K. Kellogg Foundation Logic Model Development Guide." W.K. Kellogg Foundation January, 2004. https://wkkf.issuelab.org/resource/logic-model-development-guide.html

Strategy

Martin, Roger L., and A.G. Lafley. *Playing to Win: How Strategy Really Works*. Harvard Business Review Press, 2013.

Rumelt, Richard. *Good Strategy Bad Strategy: The Difference and Why It Matters*. Crown Business, 2011.

Printed in Great Britain
by Amazon

42785314R00156